AF597672

FROM TRUNK TO TAIL

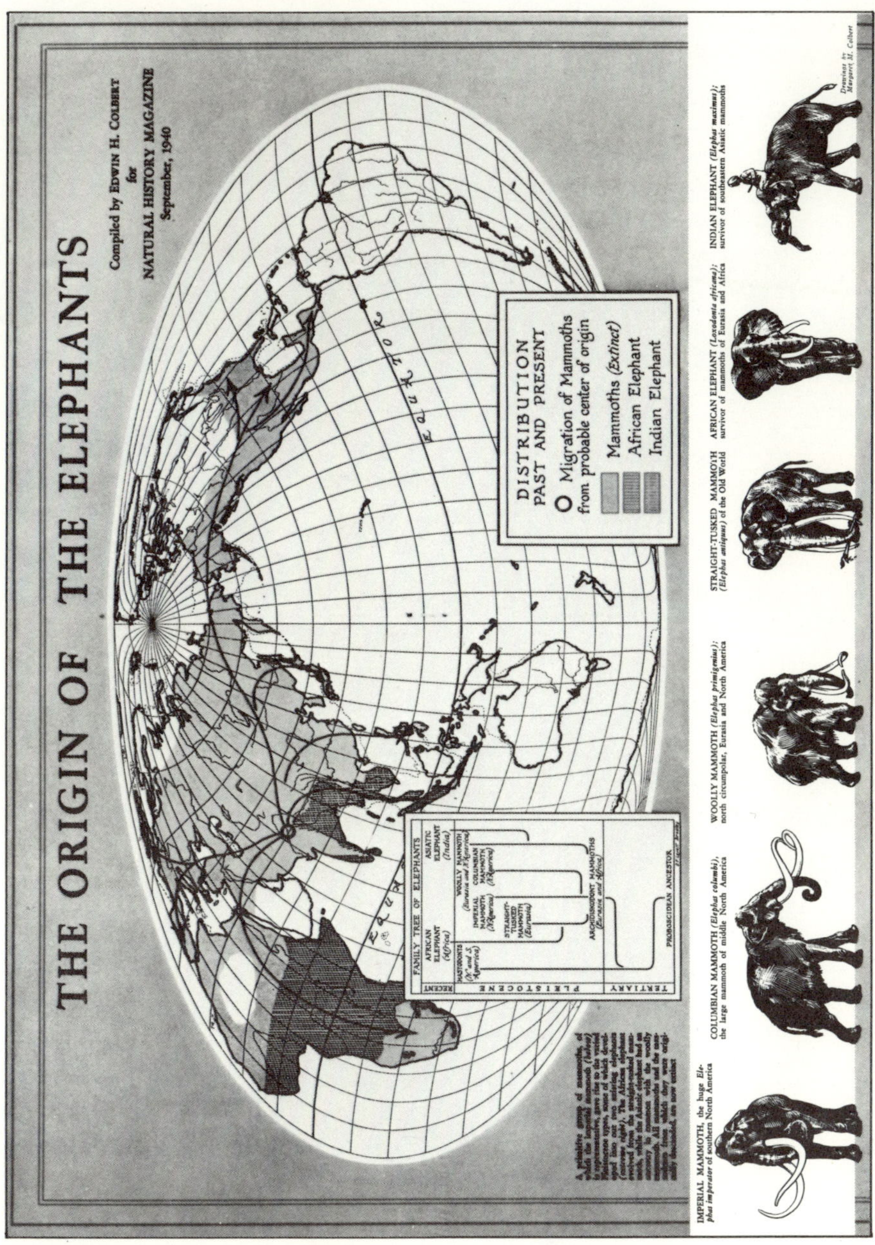

Reprinted from Natural History Magazine, September, 1940.

From Trunk to Tail

ELEPHANTS LEGENDARY and REAL

ILLUSTRATED WITH PRINTS AND PHOTOGRAPHS

SUZANNE JURMAIN

HARCOURT BRACE JOVANOVICH

NEW YORK AND LONDON

The author and publisher wish to thank the following for permission to reprint material in this book:
GERALD DUCKWORTH AND COMPANY LTD. for one verse from Hilaire Belloc's *The Bad Child's Book of Beasts.*

ALFRED A. KNOPF for "The Elephant" from *Cautionary Verses* by Hilaire Belloc. Published 1941 by Alfred A. Knopf, Inc.

THE NEW YORK TIMES for an excerpt from the article "Endangered Status Denied Elephants by U.S. Agency," May 10, 1978. © 1978 by The New York Times Company. Reprinted by permission.

Printed in the United States of America

Library of Congress Cataloging in Publication Data

Jurmain, Suzanne.
From trunk to tail.

Bibliography: p.
Includes index.
SUMMARY: Discusses the elephant's origins, habits and behavior, cooperation with man, and role in different cultures.
1. Elephants—Juvenile literature.
[1. Elephants] I. Title.
QL737.P98J87 599'.61 78-52848
ISBN 0-15-230268-9

First edition

B C D E

For Richard

The author wishes to express her thanks to MR. DAVID TRIPP for his superb assistance in matters academic, cartographic, photographic, and artistic.

Bronze coin showing a pig and an elephant, third century B.C. May commemorate a battle in which the Romans successfully used pigs to frighten war elephants belonging to their enemy, King Pyrrhus of Epirus.

Courtesy Ray Gardiner, Dept. of Coins and Medals, British Museum

Contents

a-c: Courtesy Ray Gardiner, Dept. of Coins and Medals, British Museum

a. Ancient coin showing Alexander the Great attacking Porus

b. Roman coin showing an elephant quadriga

c. Ancient coin showing Demetrius of Bactria wearing an elephant headdress

Introduction

Once, long ago, there were no elephants. But one day, the great god Brahma, creator of the world, sat looking out over the stars and thinking. In his hands he held two halves of a magical eggshell. For a long time he sat and thought and gently rubbed the eggshell with his fingertips. Then, suddenly, he had a wonderful idea. Softly, he began to sing. He sang seven holy songs, seven magical melodies. As the last note died away, a strange rumbling echoed through the universe. The eggshell in Brahma's right hand shook, and out of it stepped an enormous male elephant. Another and another followed, until eight gigantic elephants stood beside the god. Then the shell in Brahma's right hand trembled, and eight mighty female elephants stepped forth. The sixteen animals humbly bowed their heads and listened to the god's commands. Then they swiftly traveled to the corners of the world. And there they still stand, like sixteen huge pillars, holding the earth upon their backs. All other elephants are their great-grandchildren. And that is how the people of India say the first elephants were born.

Today, in the real world of twentieth-century Asia and Africa, elephants are fast disappearing. Houses, farms, factories, and cities have taken the place of the open grasslands and thick forests where these animals once roamed, and hunters are killing thousands for food and ivory. Some naturalists say that in 200 years the elephant will be extinct. If this happens, the human race will lose one of its oldest friends and finest servants. Elephants are part of our history, our folk-tales, our art, our language, and our religions. For thousands of years, people have been fascinated by these amazing creatures, and a complete encyclopedia of elephant lore would fill an elephant-size book. This book is only a beginning, an introduction to the facts, the mysteries, and the legends associated with this marvelous animal—a glimpse of what we will lose if the elephant vanishes from the earth forever.

1 In the Beginning

Scientists say that the story of the elephant family actually began in North Africa about 50 million years ago.

At that time, North Africa was a tropical paradise. There were lakes, streams, and swamps. Flowers bloomed, and tall grass covered the earth with a blanket of green. Fish swam in the waters, and many different animals made this fertile land their home. But as the centuries passed, the weather changed. The lakes and streams dried up. The animals died or migrated to better climates. Today, most of North Africa is barren, sandy desert. Only the fossils of these ancient plants and animals remain to show us what life was like so many millions of years ago.

In 1879, Georg Schweinfurth, a German traveler, discovered thousands of these fossils embedded in the rocks around Lake Moeris in Egypt. Reports of his find excited scientists, and in 1901 Dr. Charles Andrews of the British Museum mounted an expedition and traveled to Egypt to study the site himself.

Among the hundreds of fossils found and catalogued by Andrews and his assistants were the bones of an animal no one had ever seen before. For lack of a better name, the scientists called it *moeritherium,* which means "the wild animal of Lake Moeris."

"The wild animal of Lake Moeris" sounds very fierce, but actually moeritherium was nothing more than a funny, squat, fattish little beast. It had short legs and a long snout and stood about two feet tall. In fact, the kindest thing one could say about moeritherium is that it looked very much like a pig.

But it wasn't really like a pig at all. When scientists studied its skeleton carefully, they discovered that the bones in moeritherium's skull were in fact very much like an elephant's. Its feet looked like tiny elephant feet. It even had two overgrown teeth that looked like baby tusks. When the scientists added up the evidence, there was only one possible conclusion: Little moeritherium was the ancestor of all elephants!

In the millions of years that passed between the time that moeritherium munched plants in a North African swamp and modern elephants appeared on earth, the animals in the elephant family changed a great deal. Moeritherium's descendants grew bigger. They developed tusks, and, most important of all, they developed the long noses that give the elephant family its scientific name: *Proboscidea,* which means "animals with trunks."

The proboscidean family was once very large. In fact, one scientist claims that 352 different *species,* or types, of animal with trunks have lived on earth during the last 50 million years. Some of these animals were very strange indeed. There were creatures with trunks, small tusks, and gigantic lower jaws called *shovel-tuskers.* There were *woolly mammoths,* which looked like elephants with shaggy fur coats; *imperial mammoths,* fifteen feet tall—bigger than any living elephant; *mastodons,* with long twisted tusks; and many, many others.

Some of these animals lived in Africa, but many lived in Europe, Asia, North America, and South America. Millions of years ago, the continents were joined by bridges of land, and it was possible for moeritherium's descendants to travel all over the earth. At one time, animals with trunks lived on every continent except Antarctica and Australia. Though it is hard to believe, there were actually mastodons living in North America 8,000 years ago.

Then, about one million years ago, during the Ice Age, this great family of animals began to shrink. Mammoths and mastodons disappeared. The elephants living in North America, Europe, and South America vanished. Slowly, one species after another died out. What happened? Why did all these animals become extinct?

Basically, there are two probable explanations: the weather and man. We know that during the Ice Age there were great changes in the world's climate, and huge sheets of ice sometimes covered much of the earth. Mastodons, mammoths, and other prehistoric (before recorded history) elephants were enormous creatures who needed to eat hundreds of pounds of grass and leaves every day just to stay alive. If a frost or drought killed the plants, these giant animals starved. During the Ice Age, food must often have been scarce, and many of these animals probably died because they could not get enough to eat.

Those that didn't starve had to face a new enemy: man. At that time, men had only simple weapons made from bits of sharpened stone, but they were skillful hunters. They trapped and killed mammoths, reindeer, and bison. When archaeologists excavated an ancient hunter's camp at Predmost in Czechoslovakia, they found the bones of over 1,000 mammoths! In fact, ancient men killed so many mammoths that in some places houses were built with mammoth bones instead of wood. Man cannot be blamed for destroying the entire proboscidean family, but he certainly helped.

By the time the Ice Age ended (between 10,000 and 25,000 years ago), most of the proboscidean family had disappeared. Today there are only two species of elephants, and they live in only two places: Africa and Asia.

Zoologists have given these modern species scientific names. The official name for the Asiatic elephant is *Elephas maximus,* and in scientific circles the African elephant is known as *Loxodonta africana.* Scientists have given them these names because of differences in the shape of their teeth, but you don't have to look inside an animal's mouth to tell which species it belongs to. African and Asiatic elephants differ in size, shape, and personality, and because of this they have played very different roles in history.

The largest elephants live in Africa, south of the Sahara Desert. These splendid dark-gray animals have enormous ears, long ivory tusks, and two little knobs or "fingers" at the ends of their trunks. A male elephant (called a bull) is about 11 feet tall and weighs between 12,000 and 14,000 pounds. An African cow (female elephant) weighs about two tons less. Unfortunately, the African elephant's personality is not as attractive as its appearance. In captivity this handsome creature is often moody, irritable, and difficult to train. For centuries men have preferred its valuable ivory tusks to trying to cope with its unpredictable temper. Few African elephants have ever performed in the circus; but men, greedy for ivory, have hunted the African elephant almost to extinction.

The Asiatic elephants who live in India, Thailand, Burma, Ceylon, and Indonesia look like the African elephant's ugly relatives. Their light-gray skin is sometimes spotted with pink or white blotches, and their smallish ears look like ragged dishcloths. The Asiatic elephant has two large bumps on the top of its head, but only one knob or "finger" at the end of its trunk. Males generally have small tusks; females often have no tusks at all. Not only is the Asiatic elephant less elegant than the African, but it is also smaller. An Asiatic bull is about nine feet tall and weighs between 7,000 and 12,000 pounds. But despite their appearance, Asiatic elephants have earned man's love and respect. Because they are gentler, more dependable, and easier to train, Asiatic elephants have been working for man for thousands of years. They are the heroes of countless stories and myths, and in some places they have even been worshiped as gods.

African and Asiatic elephants differ in many ways, but they do have two important things in common. They are the last surviving members of the great family that began with moeritherium in North Africa so many millions of years ago, and they are two of the most extraordinary animals in the world.

"A Little Tail Behind . . ."

It isn't hard to understand why people once believed that sixteen elephants could hold up the world. Elephants are the largest animals most people have even seen. In fact, it is hard to imagine a bigger animal, even though we know that many enormous creatures have lived on earth. Millions of years before moeritherium was born, dinosaurs many times bigger than elephants ruled the world. *Brontosaurus,* for example, probably weighed about 80,000 pounds—as much as ten Asiatic elephants put together. Even now there are blue whales swimming in the ocean that weigh 150 tons and are twenty times bigger than the biggest elephant. Today, the blue whale is the largest living animal, but the elephant is the largest living animal able to walk on earth.

In the *Bad Child's Book of Beasts,* Hilaire Belloc wrote:

When people call this beast to mind,
  They marvel more and more
At such a LITTLE tail behind,
  So LARGE a trunk before.

He was absolutely right. The most fantastic thing about the elephant is its six-foot-long, 300-pound nose. This nose, this trunk, this magnificent *proboscis,* is made of skin and muscle. It wriggles and squirms like a monstrous snake. And what is a nose like that good for? The answer is: everything.

In Africa, native hunters say, "The elephant is a great lord, and his trunk is his hand." They understand perfectly.

The tip of the trunk is as sensitive as the tips of your fingers. It gives the elephant a sense of touch. By carefully feeling an object with its trunk, the animal can tell if it is hot or cold, rough or smooth.

If an elephant wants to pick something up, it uses its trunk. A trunk can pull a small tree up by the roots, pick up the tiniest peanut, or stuff food in an elephant's mouth.

But an elephant's trunk is more than a hand; it is also a splendid hose. An elephant can fill its trunk with a gallon and a half of water and squirt the water in any direction it likes—into its mouth for a drink, or over its back for a bath. Since elephants take a great many baths and drink about 50 gallons of water a day, this is a very useful accomplishment.

In 1514, Pope Leo X learned about all these talents firsthand when the king of Portugal gave him an Asiatic elephant. At that time, very few Europeans had even seen an elephant, and the Pope, his courtiers, and the people of Rome were as interested in seeing this strange animal as we would be in seeing a live dinosaur.

When the elephant arrived, the streets were crowded with curious people. The Pope sat on a balcony to get a good view, and everyone waited impatiently to see what the animal would be like.

Slowly, the elephant and its trainer moved through the narrow streets. When they reached the Pope, the trainer stopped and made the animal bow three times. The Pope was amazed. What good manners the elephant had! How clever it was! How polite! Everyone was terribly impressed. But the elephant had had enough of pomp and ceremony. He casually helped himself to a drink from a nearby trough, and a minute later His Holiness the Pope, Bishop of Rome, Vicar of Jesus Christ, Supreme Pontiff of the Universal Church, was hit in the face with a gallon of dirty water. The horrified courtiers gasped, but Leo X was a good sport. He laughed, wiped his eyes, squeezed the water out of his silk and velvet robes, and watched the elephant march majestically away.

Without a trunk, a mother elephant could not possibly take

care of her child. When the calf needs a bath, she wraps her trunk around the 200-pound baby and lifts it into the river. Then, using her nose as a combination scrub brush and shower hose, she washes it. If the calf behaves nicely, the mother cuddles and hugs it with her trunk. If the child has been naughty, it can expect a spanking. When it is time to go, the baby trots off—with its trunk wrapped tightly around its mother's tail.

The trunk also helps an elephant to communicate. A furious elephant uses its nose to make a terrible, ear-splitting scream called a "trumpet." Happy, contented elephants use their trunks to make little squeaky sounds, and one elephant greets another by putting the tip of its trunk in the other animal's mouth.

The biggest nose in the world is also one of the best. Elephants have a very keen sense of smell—and they need it. Although they have pretty eyes with long, lovely lashes, elephants cannot see very well, and they must use their noses to find food or detect danger. Often a herd of wild elephants will suddenly stop walking. All the animals stand perfectly still. Only their trunks move—back and forth like giant radar antennae. They are sniffing the air. Is it safe to go ahead? Is there food? Water? In fact, elephants have such an excellent sense of smell that hunters find it difficult to track them. Some trappers claim that when the wind is blowing in the right direction, elephants can smell a man three miles away. Others say that an elephant need only sniff a footprint to know that it was made by a man several hours before.

In ancient times, Roman soldiers trained to fight elephants were told to aim for the trunk, for in battle the trunk was a deadly weapon. Elephants have murdered men by picking them up and smashing them against rocks or trees. The same snaky nose that hugs a baby elephant can squeeze a man to jelly in no time at all.

When an elephant is born, its trunk is useless. It hangs from the calf's head like a floppy hose. The only thing the baby can do is suck the tip, as if it were a giant thumb. Three or four months pass before the elephant learns to use its wonderful nose—and then it cannot do without it.

Elephants seem to understand this and take great care of their extraordinary noses. When an elephant charges an enemy, its trunk is usually rolled up, safely out of the way. One elephant killed in a zoo fire in Dublin tried desperately to save its trunk. He dug a hole in the hard ground and buried his nose to protect it from the flames.

Not only do elephants have the biggest noses on earth, but they also have the biggest teeth. An elephant needs only four teeth to grind up its food—two on top and two on the bottom—but each tooth is more than a foot long and weighs eight or nine pounds. Elephant teeth are big, but they don't last very long. Chewing makes them wear out. When this happens, the old teeth fall out and are replaced by a new set. An elephant gets six separate sets of teeth—just enough to last a lifetime.

Elephants need their big teeth because they spend most of their lives eating. An elephant in captivity eats about 100 pounds of hay and oats a day—not to mention buns, peanuts, tobacco, and candy. A wild elephant gobbles up about 300 pounds of grass, leaves, and tree branches every twenty-four hours. This hungry animal moves across the land like a living bulldozer—uprooting bushes, knocking down trees, trampling crops, and leaving a ruined landscape behind. Because of their enormous appetites and destructive eating habits, most people do not want wild elephants for neighbors. In Africa, loggers get angry because elephants destroy valuable mahogany trees. Farmers in Asia and Africa have been at war with elephants for centuries because the animals can eat great quantities of the coconuts, mangoes, bananas, berries, and sugar cane growing in the fields. Whenever there are elephants in the vicinity, farmers frantically shake rattles, beat drums, and light fires to try to keep the animals away.

One of the reasons elephants need so much food is that their big teeth are not very efficient. In 1935 a scientist named Dr. Francis Benedict discovered this by doing an experiment to find out how much food elephants actually chew up and digest.

First he took the inner tube from an old tire and cut it into rectangles and diamond-shaped pieces. Then he hid these rubber tidbits in loaves of bread and fed the bread to two elephants at the Franklin Park Zoo in Boston. They happily gobbled up these peculiar sandwiches, not at all bothered by the pieces of rubber.

For the next day or so, the zoo keepers checked the elephants' droppings carefully. To everyone's amazement, they found most of the rubber cutouts—without a tooth mark on them.

As a result of his experiments, Dr. Benedict concluded that an elephant actually needs less than half the food it eats. In other words, if a wild elephant eats 300 pounds of food, it digests about 132 pounds and leaves 168 pounds of waste.

All animals have different kinds of teeth for different jobs. Some teeth are used for grinding, while others are used to cut the food apart. These cutting teeth are called *incisors,* and an elephant's long, splendid tusks are really nothing more than giant, overgrown incisors.

Many Asiatic bulls have tusks that are five feet long. Both male and female African elephants have tusks that sometimes grow to be eight feet. The British Museum has an enormous pair of African tusks that weighs 440 pounds!

Young elephants have tiny incisors called "milk tusks." These baby teeth are only two inches long and fall out before the calf is two years old. After that, real tusks start to grow—and keep on growing for the rest of the animal's life.

A wild elephant uses its strong, pointed tusks to dig up trees and vegetables. In Burma, working elephants learn to use their tusks to move logs, and sometimes trainers saw off the tips so that these enormous teeth will grow bigger and thicker. When an elephant is angry or has been attacked, tusks can become deadly weapons—twin spears that can stab a tiger, another elephant, or even a man.

Oddly enough, elephants without tusks never seem to miss them. They often develop bigger trunks instead, and in a fight the one without tusks may be the winner, because his longer, wider, stronger trunk can smash those overgrown teeth to splinters.

Actually, men seem to value tusks more than elephants do. Tusks are made of ivory, and this beautiful white substance has been used and treasured for thousands of years. Even the name "elephant" comes from the Greek word *eléphas,* which means "ivory."

But if an elephant's tusks are magnificent and its nose is incredible, its body is ridiculous! The skin sags into a million wrinkles. The few prickly hairs scattered about its body make the animal look like a worn-out scrub brush. Even the bunch of hair at the tip of the tail looks like an afterthought.

Sometimes elephants are called *pachyderms,* which means they are animals with thick skins. It is a good description, for the skin on many parts of an elephant's body is about one inch thick. This thick skin should be as tough as armor, but it isn't. Elephants are ticklish. Their thick skins are horribly sensitive, and flies and mosquitoes make them absolutely miserable. The skin should protect the elephant, but actually the opposite is true—the elephant has to spend a lot of time protecting its skin.

An elephant usually takes at least one bath a day, to keep its skin clean and soft. Then, as soon as it gets out of the water, it rolls in the mud and powders itself with dirt. When the mud dries, it forms a thick crust that protects the animal from troublesome insects. Unfortunately, this protection is only temporary. After a while, the mud cracks, the elephant gets itchy—and it is time for another bath.

Elephants don't mind bathing. They like water and are excellent swimmers, and will paddle happily in a lake, pool, pond, or puddle. Some have even traveled long distances by water. In 1950 elephant expert J. H. Williams reported in his book, *Elephant Bill,* that an elephant had gone swimming in the Bay of Bengal. This bay, which separates India and Burma, is dotted with islands. The adventurous animal simply swam from one to another—sometimes crossing a mile of ocean on the way.

Although there are many stories about elephants swimming across deep rivers and climbing mountains, it is hard to believe that these huge, clumsy-looking beasts can move at all. In fact, hundreds of years ago, Europeans who had seen elephants only in books thought elephants couldn't bend their legs because they had no knees! That, of course, is nonsense. Elephants are a lot more athletic than they look. They can kneel, walk, and even run. Generally, they take it easy and stroll along at about six miles an hour, but if something frightens an elephant, it will take off like a freight train and gallop away at a speed of 18 to 25 miles an hour. That may not sound very fast, but remember that a racehorse, which is one-twelfth the size of an elephant, can run only twice as fast. However, elephants were not built for racing. Galloping tires them out, and no elephant can keep it up for very long.

Although elephants can run, they can't jump. Because of the way their bones are put together, they can't manage even the smallest bounce without injuring their legs.

Elephants may not be able to leap over ditches, but they can climb mountains very well. Sure-footed, slow, and steady, they can easily travel over narrow, rocky ledges. The trunk can even be wrapped around boulders and used like a mountaineer's rope. If the slope is very steep, the elephant simply sits on its hindquarters and slides down. In addition, elephants easily adapt to the chilly mountain air. During his experiments, Dr. Benedict discovered that elephants were comfortable at a chilly 40° F. In Kenya, travelers have sometimes seen elephants wandering through the mountains when the temperature was well below freezing.

Although no elephant will ever win a beauty contest, its peculiar-looking body is really practical and well designed. The legs look clumsy, but they are thick and strong enough to support the animal's great weight, and nimble enough to allow the elephant to climb mountains, ford rivers, and travel over endless miles of forest and plain in its search for food. The tusks are excellent digging tools and weapons. The trunk allows this huge animal to eat and drink without the awkwardness and inconvenience of kneeling down or climbing trees. Even the ugly, sensitive skin is thick enough to keep the elephant warm in cold climates.

Only the elephant's great size is a problem. Today, because of its huge appetite and destructive eating habits, the elephant is in danger. A cockroach can live on a crumb, but elephants need enormous feeding grounds—and these feeding grounds are rapidly disappearing. Each year more of the wilderness is cleared away and more of the elephants' ancient homeland vanishes. Even in the great national parks established to protect endangered wildlife, these animals are not safe. Thousands of elephants looking for new homes have crowded into these parks and thousands more have been born inside the gates. The parks have become overcrowded, and the result has been disaster. At Tsavo National Park in Kenya huge herds of hungry elephants knocked down the trees, ate the grass, gobbled up the bushes, and turned the park into a wasteland. Soon there was not enough food to go around, and thousands of elephants died of starvation. In some wildlife preserves game wardens have coped with these catastrophic conditions by hiring hunters to thin out the herds, and many conservationists feel that it is better to shoot some animals than to allow all of them to starve slowly.

Unfortunately, there is no easy solution to this problem. There is a limited amount of room on earth, and both people and elephants need food and living space. The elephant is one of the wonders of nature, but many people are wondering sadly if there is enough room for these hungry giants on our overcrowded planet.

Life Style

Imagine carrying a growing baby inside you for almost two years before it is born. It sounds incredible, but that is what elephants actually do.

When the time to deliver the baby finally comes, the mother chooses a nice shady spot. Then, with the help of another female elephant, she gives it a good cleaning. Sticks, stones, and bits of brush are carefully swept away, and the two elephants trample the dirt so it will be soft and loose. When the housekeeping is finished, the mother and her friend have nothing to do but wait.

At last, a three-foot-tall, 200-pound baby elephant is born. It is a hairy, helpless little creature that cannot walk, run, or fight. After half an hour, the calf can stand on wobbly legs long enough to drink its mother's milk, but it will be two days before it will be able to walk well enough to keep up with the older elephants.

The mother and her friend, called an "auntie," take care of the child together. They bathe the baby, cuddle it, scold it, and, above all, protect it. Lots of wild animals like the taste of elephant meat, and although elephants are good fighters, tigers kill one out of every four baby elephants in Asia.

If the mother dies, the auntie will care for the baby as if it were her own. If the auntie is killed, another female elephant will take her place. Elephants seem to like being mothers, and females are always happy to adopt a child—even a human one.

Ivan Sanderson, the author of a book about elephants called the *Dynasty of Abu,* learned about elephant mothers at a very early age. When Mr. Sanderson was a little boy, his nanny often took him to the zoo. One day, while they were watching the animals, a female elephant suddenly wrapped her trunk around the child, picked him up, and kidnapped him. The elephant had the most motherly intentions. She treated the child as if he were an elephant calf, and tucked him safely between her front legs. Mr. Sanderson's nanny, however, had rather different ideas about child care. She bravely marched up to the elephant, smacked it with her umbrella, and snatched the child away from the startled beast.

In the wild, an elephant mother keeps a sharp eye on her children, and little calves are never allowed to wander far from her side. Even trained elephants do not like being separated from their families, and in Burmese lumber camps elephants are allowed to take their calves to work. While the mothers haul logs, the calves chase birds, play in the leaves, tease the older elephants, and generally make pests of themselves. The mothers scold and fuss, but if a calf gets into real trouble, its mother immediately goes to the rescue.

J. H. Williams tells the story of an elephant named Ma Shwe (which means "Miss Gold") who actually risked her life to save her child.

Ma Shwe worked in a lumber camp in Burma, and like the other working mothers, she kept her calf close at her side. One day the river near the camp flooded, and before anyone realized what was happening, Ma Shwe's three-month-old calf was swept away by the rushing waters. The little elephant struggled and tried to swim, but the current was very strong and it could barely keep its head above the water. As soon as Ma Shwe saw this, she plunged into the river, grabbed the drowning child with her trunk, lifted it out of the river, and placed it on a rocky ledge. The child was safe—but Ma Shwe was in terrible danger. The flood rushed furiously on, and several times the huge elephant was almost carried away by the swirling waters. After a long, hard fight, she finally reached the bank and dragged herself out of the river. Both elephants were safe, but Ma Shwe was on one side of the river, and the lonely, wet, frightened little calf was on the other. There was no earthly way to get safely across. For hours and hours Ma Shwe stood and watched the flood. But as soon as the water began to go down and it was safe, she swam over to be with her child.

An elephant mother does many things for her child—she loves it and cares for it, but most important, she teaches it how to survive. Some animals are born with a great deal of knowledge already wired into their brains. No one has to teach birds, fish, or reptiles how to behave, where to lay eggs, or when to fly south for the winter. Their *instincts* tell them how to do these things. Elephants, however, are born knowing very little, and they must depend on adults to teach them how to behave and how to survive. These lessons take years, and an elephant is not considered a grownup until it is about twenty years old.

In the wild, a baby elephant has many teachers, because mothers, fathers, aunts, uncles, and cousins live together in herds of ten to fifty animals. People in some parts of Africa believe that each herd has a king—a very grand bull with a bevy of female elephant servants who clean his tusks, brush the mud off his back, and bring him food. It's a good story, but it isn't true. Actually, elephant society is *matriarchal*—which means that each herd has a very distinguished female leader. She is the oldest, biggest, strongest female in the group, and she acts as a mother, a queen, and a general. At the very first sign of danger, the other animals crowd around her. If she decides to run, they follow. If she decides to attack, the cows will charge with her—although the bulls may run away and leave the females to do the fighting.

A herd of wild elephants never stays in one spot for very long. Since ten wild elephants can eat about 3,000 pounds of food a day, they have to keep moving. If the herd stayed in one place, the animals would starve.

Because wild elephants have to travel, they usually lead a well-organized life. In Burma, for instance, elephants spend the months from June to October eating bamboo in the hills and then come down to the valleys to eat grass. Year after year each herd travels the same way, and the paths they have worn through the jungle are so clear that a man can easily find them. In fact, Sir Halford Mackinder, the first man to climb Mt. Kenya, spent long, frustrating days trying to cut his way through the thick African underbrush until, to his delight, he discovered that elephant trails were easier to follow.

The elephants in a herd travel together, eat together, bring up their children together, and care for each other. If one animal is hurt, the others come to the rescue. If one has trouble walking, another offers a shoulder to lean on. Zoo animals sometimes develop special friendships, and sometimes adult elephants fall in love.

The world's greatest elephant love story was recorded by Baron Cuvier, a famous French zoologist. He actually knew the lovers, two elephants named Hans and Parkie, when they lived in the Paris zoo in the 1790s.

Hans and Parkie had spent a good part of their lives together. They had traveled from Asia to Holland, and from Holland to Paris, and it was quite plain to everyone that they adored each other and could not bear to be apart. They lived happily in the Paris zoo, until Hans suddenly caught pneumonia and died. The grief was almost more than Parkie could bear. She moped. She mourned. She even stopped eating. The zoo officials tried to cheer her up, but each day Parkie just looked thinner and sadder. Time passed, and the keepers began to worry. They were so afraid Parkie would die of loneliness that they decided to find her a new friend. Since there weren't any elephants available, they introduced her to a camel. Parkie glared scornfully. How could they expect a well-bred elephant to like an ugly beast with a humpy back? She suffered on alone until, at last, the zoo proudly presented her with a new male elephant. But Parkie wasn't interested. She was still deeply attached to Hans, and no other elephant could take his place. Nothing could console her, and she finally died of grief the following year.

Although very few elephants are as devoted as Hans and Parkie, they generally are friendly, affectionate creatures. They are not quarrelsome and seldom fight among themselves. Occasionally two bulls will battle over a cow until one of them is killed, but female elephants are better behaved. When a cow gets cross with another elephant, she simply gives it a sharp slap or shove. Although some captive elephants are afraid of small animals and dislike dogs and horses, wild elephants don't start fights, and few animals are foolish enough to quarrel with them. But if another animal should attack, an elephant will fight fiercely to defend itself and its family.

A circus elephant may panic because a dog barks or a rabbit runs across its path, but only a *rogue* elephant will attack without any reason at all. Rogues live alone, probably because other animals object to their wild, violent behavior. Because they will attack and kill anything that moves without warning, rogues are a danger to all around them. No one really knows why some elephants behave this way. Perhaps they are suffering from a terribly painful wound or disease. Perhaps they have simply gone mad. Unfortunately, there is only one cure: A rogue must be shot before it does serious damage.

Luckily, very few elephants become rogues, but there are times when even the friendliest, tamest, gentlest male elephant turns into a raging monster. When a dark, smelly, oily liquid begins to ooze from a gland located between its eye and ear, people had better be careful. The elephant is on *musth.*

This state of temporary insanity may last anywhere from two weeks to two months. As soon as it is over, the elephant stops misbehaving and goes back to being its old friendly, obedient self. Although it sounds like a disease, musth is actually a normal part of a healthy bull elephant's life. Some animals go on musth every six months; others may go two or three years without having an attack. A male usually comes on musth for the first time when he is fifteen to twenty years old, and by the time an elephant reaches the age of forty-five or fifty, it may stop having these attacks altogether. Scientists once thought that musth had something to do with mating. They now know that isn't the explanation, but they still have not discovered the right answer.

As soon as the musth period starts, the bull must be caged or chained. For a while the animal may stand perfectly still, staring blankly into space. Then, suddenly, it goes mad—screaming, thrashing, kicking, and smashing everything in sight. The frenzied creature refuses to eat, is too restless to sleep, and will attack anyone who comes near—even a trainer it has known and loved for years. While they are in this state, elephants are incredibly dangerous. In the late nineteenth century a circus elephant suddenly went on musth and escaped from its trainer. It dashed through the streets of Troy, New York, like a tornado. People were trampled, hurled into the air, and smashed against walls. Aside from the personal injuries, the elephant did $4,000 worth of damage before it was finally killed.

Actually, we have only just began to learn about elephants. Before the beginning of the twentieth century, scientists knew very little about these animals. It was hard to study wild elephants because they lived in remote, dangerous places. Because it was difficult and expensive to transport the animals, there were very few elephants in circuses and zoos. Since there were no available facts, all sorts of tall tales sprang up about these elusive beasts. According to these legends, elephants were extraordinarily intelligent animals who lived for hundreds of years and went to special secret places to die. Because these stories were so old and because so many people believed them, many modern scientists were intrigued. They wanted to find out if these stories were true or not.

In 1957, one of these scientists, Professor Bernard Rensch of the University of Münster in Germany, decided to find out if elephants were really smart, so he made up an intelligence test for them.

Professor Rensch showed a young Asiatic elephant two boxes. One box had a circle on top; the other had a square. Whenever the animal pointed to the square, it was given food. When it pointed to the circle, nothing happened. The professor wanted to find out how long it would take the elephant to learn the difference between the two boxes. A human being could figure it out after three or four tries, but it took the elephant 330 tries to learn this simple fact.

An elephant's brain weighs ten pounds; a man's weighs only three pounds. Why is a man smarter? Part of the answer is that an elephant's body is 500 to 1,000 times bigger than its brain. A man's body is only 40 to 50 times bigger. An elephant has to use more of its brain to manage its body. A man doesn't need as much brain to make his smaller body work—which is why he has plenty of brain left over for "thinking."

Professor Rensch's experiment showed that elephants are certainly not the smartest animals on earth—but they are far from stupid. It takes a very intelligent animal to use a stone or branch as a tool, but Iain Douglas-Hamilton, who studied wild elephants in

Africa, once saw an elephant use a twig as a back-scratcher. Sometimes elephants actually seem to be smarter than human beings. Several years ago, two baby elephants escaped from a circus in Oklahoma and hid so well that dozens of people equipped with planes, dogs, horses, and cars couldn't find them. Finally, the circus trainers decided that only another elephant would be clever enough to pick up their trail.

Elephants may not be as wise as people once thought, but scientists have discovered that the old stories are right about one thing—elephants never forget. At least, almost never. Elephants remember circus tricks they haven't done for years. They remember people who were kind, and those who were cruel. Although it took Professor Rensch's elephant a long time to learn the difference between a circle and a square, it did remember its lesson. When the elephant took the same test a year later, it scored almost 100 percent.

Although there is some truth in the tall tales about an elephant's intelligence and memory, the idea that elephants can live for hundreds of years is absolutely nonsense.

Through careful research, scientists have discovered that elephants in captivity live to be about sixty years old. The oldest elephant on record is a female Asiatic elephant named Jessie who celebrated her sixty-ninth birthday at the zoo in Sydney, Australia. Wild elephants probably don't live very much longer, because elephants lose their last teeth when they are about sixty years old, and a wild elephant without teeth would starve.

Even after the facts about an elephant's life span were known, many people continued to believe the old legend. In his book, *Elephants,* Richard Carrington explains how this ridiculous old story almost caused an international problem.

In 1798, General Napoleon Bonaparte left France to conquer Egypt. While Napoleon was camped on the banks of the Nile, a Turkish governor gave him an elephant. Since the general didn't really need the animal, he simply shipped it off to France. The elephant arrived safely and would have been perfectly happy to stay in its new home—but Napoleon had other plans. He decided to give it to the Emperor Francis of Austria. So the poor elephant was packed up again, shipped to Vienna, and placed in the Imperial Menagerie. After a few years, the elephant had become very bad-tempered. The Austrians didn't want the nasty beast, so they sent it on to a zoo in Budapest, Hungary. That was the last anyone heard of it, until 1930. Then a strange story began to go around. People were saying that the elephant living in the Budapest zoo in 1930 was actually the same elephant Napoleon had sent to France 132 years before.

Because Napoleon was a great French hero, the French, quite naturally, felt that his elephant should live in France. This resulted in an enormous diplomatic fuss. The French insisted it was *their* elephant. The Hungarians replied that it certainly was not. Finally, both parties agreed to let an expert settle the business once and for all. At their request, Mr. Stanley S. Flower, a world-famous authority on elephants, studied the problem and examined the records. His findings made the French look very silly: He proved beyond the shadow of a doubt that the Budapest elephant was only forty years old!

Of all these legends, the myth about elephant graveyards is probably the most intriguing. People once believed that old elephants went to a special, secret place to die. Travelers claim to have seen these places, and there are all sorts of fantastic stories about them. One of the most famous comes from the story of the "Seventh Voyage of Sinbad the Sailor" in the *Arabian Nights*.

Sinbad the Sailor, a hardy old adventurer, was on his way home from a visit to the Kingdom of Serendib, when a band of pirates suddenly attacked his ship. Most of the crew died in the fighting, but Sinbad and a few others were taken prisoner and later sold as slaves. Sinbad was purchased by a rich merchant who soon put him to work. The old sailor was given a bow and arrows, taken to a large forest, and told to sit in a tree and shoot elephants as they went past. There were dozens of elephants; Sinbad was an excellent marksman, and soon the delighted merchant had a great many ivory tusks to sell in the market. For a time all went well, but one day, instead of walking by as usual, the elephants turned and charged straight toward Sinbad. The largest elephant pulled the tree up by the roots, grabbed the terrified sailor, and carried him off. After a little while, the huge elephant stopped and set Sinbad gently on the ground. The startled man caught his breath and looked around. He was standing in the middle of an elephant cemetery. The entire hillside was covered with bones and tusks!

The elephants, of course, were wise enough to know that men only wanted ivory, and clever enough to think of a way to save their own lives. The ivory from the elephant's graveyard made the merchant rich, Sinbad was given his freedom, and the elephants were allowed to live in peace.

People continued to believe stories like this because occasionally many elephant skeletons are found in one place. Are these real elephant cemeteries? Scientists say no. In a real cemetery, most of the bones would belong to very old elephants. But when scientists examined these groups of skeletons, they found the bones of young, old, and middle-aged elephants all mixed together. They concluded that these were actually the skeletons of a herd of elephants who died of a disease or were killed in some disaster.

Although scientists have explained away the myth of elephant graveyards, they cannot explain why elephants are fascinated with death. A mother elephant may carry the body of a dead calf with her for days. The animals in a herd may tenderly bury the body of a dead comrade under a pile of branches, leaves, and dirt. People have even seen living elephants carrying a dead animal's bones and tusks.

The things that elephants do often baffle scientists, and it is no wonder that ordinary people once made up so many stories about them. In the forests of Africa and Asia and in countless zoos all over the world, people are studying elephants. Each year they learn a little more. Perhaps one day they will find the real reasons for some of this puzzling behavior, and we will truly understand why elephants act as they do.

4

The Elephant as Prey

When you see elephants dancing in a circus ring or ambling peacefully across an open plain, it's hard to believe the hunter's warning: Elephants are the most dangerous animals in the world. They are difficult to track and to kill, and an elephant attack is swift and deadly.

Despite the danger, men have been hunting elephants for thousands of years. In this deadly contest, the hunter's best weapon is his brain. The elephant is bigger, but the hunter is more intelligent. If the man hopes to kill the animal, he will have to outsmart it.

The easiest way to outsmart an animal is to build a trap. Even prehistoric men who hunted mammoths with stone-tipped spears knew how to make traps, and they drew pictures of them on the walls of their caves. These ancient traps were very efficient. In fact one of them, the pitfall, worked so well that people are still using it today.

Making a pitfall is easy. First the hunters look for a path that elephants often use. Then they dig a deep hole in the middle of the trail. The sides of the hole slant inward and come to a point at the bottom. Branches, leaves, and dirt are piled over the opening. The idea, of course, is to make everything look so natural that the animal will never guess the trap is there. Once the pitfall has been made, the hunters wait.

A bull passes by, his trunk swinging close to the ground. He sniffs. The leaves have a funny smell. They have been touched by men, and he senses that something is wrong. He steps carefully around the hole. No other elephants pass by that day.

The hunters wait.

The next day two cows and a calf walk toward the trap. The mother elephant is waving her trunk in the air. She pats the calf. She sniffs for food. She is not paying any attention to the path in front of her. Crash! She falls into the pit. She trumpets and struggles, but she cannot climb the steep slanting walls. The other cow tries to help, but there is nothing she can do. Finally, she takes the victim's calf away.

The hunters return. They are delighted. Their trap has worked. They throw their spears, kill the animal, and that night they feast on elephant meat.

Of course, it doesn't always happen like that. Some tribesmen claim that if an elephant finds a pitfall and doesn't get caught, it considerately removes the cover so that other animals will be able to avoid the trap.

A pitfall is a good way to catch one elephant. Suppose, however, the hunters want ivory and need to kill a lot of elephants at once. They need a different kind of trap, and they might consider using fire.

To make this trap work, the hunters must wait until they find a large herd of elephants together. Then they quickly set fire to bushes and twigs. In a few minutes, the elephants are prisoners in a ring of fire. Blinded and choking from the smoke, half crazy with fear of the flames, they try to run. The hunters, of course, are waiting. As the terrified animals break through the fiery circle, they are slaughtered with spears.

Not all elephants are caught in traps. There are other ways to outsmart an elephant, but all of them require great courage and skill.

In parts of Zaïre, a tribesman goes elephant hunting alone. He is naked, because even the smallest piece of clothing might catch on a branch and give him away. He smears his body with dung so that the elephant won't recognize the smell of a human. His only weapon is a heavy spear.

Moving with utmost care, he tracks his prey through forest,

brush, and open fields. He follows, waits, and follows again. When the elephant stops to rest, the hunter strikes. Swiftly he thrusts his spear deep into the elephant's belly—and runs for his life. In a flash the furious, wounded animal comes thundering after him. *If* the hunter is a fast runner and *if* he has stabbed the animal in the right place, the elephant will be able to follow him only a little way. Once it falls and is dead, the hunter can return to claim his prize.

Two hundred years ago, Ethiopian men hunted elephants another way. At that time, Ethiopia was a wild, uncivilized country. People thought nothing of cutting steaks off a live cow or making necklaces out of the flesh of dead enemies. Brutality was part of their lives, and elephants were hunted in a way that was both clever and cruel.

Ethiopian hunters worked in pairs. There were two men and a horse. One man held the reins, and the other sat behind holding a sharp-edged sword. As soon as they found an elephant, the game began. Spurring the horse to a furious pace, they galloped round and round the elephant while the rider yelled: "I am such and such a man; this is my horse that has such a name; I killed your father in such a place, and your grandfather in such another; and I am now come to kill you: you are but an ass in comparison to them!"*

Around and around they went, shouting and screaming insults. The astonished elephant could not have understood the words, but it didn't like the noise or the harassment. As the teasing went on, the elephant grew angrier and angrier. Finally, it began to lash at the rider with its trunk. The furious elephant was so intent on getting rid of the screaming rider that it never saw the swordsman slip to the ground. Suddenly there was a sharp pain. The swordsman had slashed the back of the animal's leg. With one blow he had sliced through the tendon that attaches the leg muscle to the heel. The elephant was crippled. The fight was over. The hunters could kill the miserable creature or simply wait until it bled to death.

Today, even though elephants are hunted with guns, the pursuit still isn't easy. Sometimes it takes a hunter several days to track an elephant. He can wait through long, hot, thirsty hours for just the right moment—and then miss. A skillful hunter will try to put a bullet through the animal's brain. A less experienced one will aim for the

* Charles Andersson, *The Lion and the Elephant,* p. 360.

heart. Whichever shot he chooses, the hunter must take care. He must kill with his first bullet. A wounded elephant will attack, and the unlucky hunter probably will not live to tell the tale.

Because of the danger, hunters often feel they need luck just as much as they need their wits and their weapons. Some hunters say their prayers, some carry lucky charms, others have tried to use magic.

The first people to try hunting with magic lived in prehistoric times—about 50,000 years ago. For these men, hunting was a serious business. They had to kill or starve. They made traps, but the traps didn't always work. Their weapons were crude spears tipped with sharp pieces of flint. It is no wonder they felt the need for a little magical help.

Deep inside their dark caves, they drew pictures of the animals they hunted—bison, reindeer, and mammoths—probably because they thought the paintings gave them magical control over the world. Perhaps they thought that if they drew thousands of animals, game would be plentiful. Perhaps they thought that by drawing pictures of successful hunters, they could help real hunters kill their prey. They may have tried other kinds of magic, too. We can't be sure, but we do know that today, 50,000 years later, some people still believe in hunting magic.

In Africa, south of the Sahara Desert, lives a tribe of people called the Mindassa. They understand that elephant hunters need special skills, special training, and special magic. The man in charge of the magic is a witch doctor called *Njanga djoko.*

Before the hunt begins, *Njanga djoko* spends a whole day praying in a hut filled with guns, spears, the bones of former witch doctors, and parts of dead elephants. Once he has finished his prayers, other ceremonies begin. First, he slaughters a sheep and some hens, and smears the blood on the bones of his ancestors. After the sacrifice, the elephant hunters solemnly gather and feast on meat from the animals *Njanga djoko* has killed. Then, when evening comes, a great dance is held in the village. Everyone dances—including the hunters, who with slow, measured steps act out the part of the huge beast they are planning to kill. The next morning the hunt begins.

Led by *Njanga djoko,* the men set out to track the elephant. When the witch doctor feels the time is right, he hurls his spear or fires his gun. The other hunters follow. If their aim is good, and the magic has been performed correctly, the elephant will soon be dead.

Once the hunt is over, the hardest part of the witch doctor's job begins. He has to cut off the elephant's tail, run back to the village, pick up his wife, and hurry back to the elephant. When he returns to the carcass, he cuts off the tip of the trunk. Pressing it to his mouth, he sucks some of the blood, then passes it to his wife, so she can do the same.

After this the meat is divided up. The witch doctor gets the liver, intestines, trunk, and part of the heart. Some of this he will eat; some will be put away so it can be used as a magic charm in the next hunt.

At long last the hunters sit down to eat, drink, and celebrate. Everyone has a marvelous time—everyone except *Njanga djoko.* He cannot join in the feasting because he must mourn for the elephant. If no one grieves, the elephant's spirit will be angry, and an angry spirit could hurt every man, woman, and child in the village. So the witch doctor moans and weeps and sings of his sadness. The amount of time *Njanga djoko* spends weeping and wailing depends on the size of the elephant. The spirit of a little elephant is not very dangerous, so *Njanga djoko* cries only a little bit. But a big elephant can do a lot of damage, and it takes a lot of tears to set its spirit to rest.

Only after all this is finished can the tired witch doctor eat his dinner and go to bed to rest up for the next hunt.

Most chefs think that elephant meat is rather tough and smelly. But according to some people, a properly prepared elephant foot is a dish fit for a king. The following recipe for savory roast elephant foot was recommended by Mr. Charles Andersson.

Ingredients: 1 elephant foot
salt
pepper
vinegar
oil

First, dig a hole four feet deep and build a fire in it. Wait four or five hours until the coals are hot; then place the foot carefully on the coals.

Cover the hole with green wood. Cover the wood with wet grass. Cover the grass with a thick layer of mud. Cook thirty hours or more.
When the foot is completely cooked, peel off the bottom. Sprinkle the meat with vinegar, salt, and pepper and serve.

Kings, emperors, presidents, and adventurers have been excited by the challenge of hunting these dangerous animals. Even Egyptian pharaohs went hunting. In fact, when King Thutmose III of Egypt went elephant hunting 3,000 years ago, it almost changed the course of history.

Thutmose was a little man with a big nose. He was a fine king and a good general, and when he wanted to relax, he liked to go hunting.

One day Thutmose and his friends were galloping along the banks of the river when they saw a huge herd of elephants. Thutmose was delighted. He thought he would slaughter the elephants as easily as he conquered cities. But something went wrong. The largest animal suddenly charged the king. People screamed, but the animal came thundering on. Thutmose couldn't escape. The animal was almost on top of him when one of his courtiers courageously attacked the charging elephant. With one blow of his sword he cut off the animal's trunk and saved the life of his king. A very grateful Thutmose rewarded him with gold and precious stones. The courtier, whose name was Amen-en Heb, became a rich and honored man. But there is no record of how Thutmose felt about elephant hunting after that.

For centuries men armed with everything from guns to magic charms have been the elephant's worst enemies. During the Ice Age, prehistoric men helped kill the last of the mammoths. Since then, hunters have slaughtered animals so ruthlessly that by 1900 the African elephant was almost extinct.

Some of these animals were killed by sportsmen. Some were killed by hunters looking for food. Most died because men wanted ivory.

Ivory is beautiful and valuable. Prehistoric men carved needles, statues, and fishhooks out of mammoth tusks. Since then people have paid fabulous sums for ivory cages, doors, chairs, jewelry, book covers, dice, walking sticks, billiard balls, piano keys, combs, brushes, knife handles, cups, and musical instruments. King Ahab of Israel had an ivory house. The Roman emperor Caligula built an ivory stable for his horse. African kings had ivory house posts. European ladies fanned themselves with ivory fans. The artists of India, China, and Japan became famous for their exquisite ivory carvings. The ancient Greeks thought that one of the seven wonders of the world was the ivory statue of Zeus at Olympia. Carved by the famous sculptor Pheidias, this statue was 58 feet tall and made of wood covered with a thin layer of ivory. People who saw it claimed the statue was so beautifully carved and painted that it seemed to be alive. Even today, shops are crowded with beads, boxes, statues, and chess pieces made of ivory.

Unfortunately, the best and most beautiful ivory in the world comes from the tusks of the African elephant.

In ancient times, huge herds of elephants lived in North Africa, but there are no elephants in North Africa today. Ivory hunters killed them all. By A.D. 400 the North African elephant was extinct, and hunters had already begun to attack the great herds that lived south of the Sahara Desert. The invention of guns made killing easier, and in the nineteenth century ivory hunting became big business. Between 1870 and 1881, 5,286 *tons* of ivory were shipped to England alone. By the beginning of the twentieth century, there were very few African elephants left.

When government officials in Africa realized the elephant was in danger of becoming extinct, they took action at once. Laws were passed limiting the number of elephants a hunter could shoot. National parks and wildlife preserves were established. Sportsmen were asked to shoot elephants with cameras instead of guns. A tremendous amount of time, effort, and money was poured into this attempt to save the African elephant, and after a few years the work began to pay off. The number of animals increased, and soon herds of elephants were once again roaming through the African forests and plains.

Unfortunately, the story doesn't have a happy ending. Today, the African elephant is in danger again. This time the animals are being attacked by an army of hunters who deliberately choose to break the law. These hunters, or *poachers,* kill for two reasons: food and money. In most parts of Africa, a man can make more money by killing an elephant and selling the tusks than he can make by working at his job for a whole year. Tribesmen, long accustomed to killing elephants and other animals for meat, think the hunting laws are unfair, so they ignore them. But the worst criminals are dishonest government officials. Poaching is making them rich. They buy tusks from poachers, sell the ivory, and pocket the cash. Because they are making so much money out of the illegal ivory trade, these officials don't enforce the hunting laws. Very few poachers are caught, and very few are punished. The results of this are frightening. In Meru National Park, poachers kill 100 elephants every year. There are so many poachers at Tsavo National Park that the wardens find dead and dying animals every day.

Some people are trying to solve this problem. In Kenya, for example, the government recently banned all hunting and made it illegal to sell elephant tusks, zebra hides, rhinocerous horns, and other animal trophies. These new laws should help, but past experience has shown that even good laws are useless unless people enforce them. People have to care enough to make the laws work. If people do not care, all the laws and good intentions in the world cannot save the African elephant from destruction.

From *A Guide to the Elephants (recent and fossil) Exhibited in the British Museum* (Natural History), 1922. Courtesy of the Trustees of the British Museum (Natural History)

Moeritherium: the ancestor of all elephants

From *The Ivory King*, Charles F. Holder, Scribner's, New York, 1886

Hunters attack an elephant with swords

From *The Ivory King*, Charles F. Holder, Scribner's, New York, 1886

Hunting a mammoth

From *Un Hiver au Cambodge*, Edgar Boulanger, Mame et Fils, Tours, 1887

The dangers of elephant hunting

From *The Ivory King*, Charles F. Holder, Scribner's, New York, 1886

An old print showing a herd of wild elephants.
Adults eat grass while a mother nurses her calf.

From *The Ivory King*, Charles F. Holder, Scribner's, New York, 1886

Female Asiatic elephant and her calf. One elephant often greets another by putting the tip of its trunk into the other animal's mouth.

Courtesy Barbara Lucas

African elephant with missing right tusk

Asiatic elephant

New York Zoological Society Photo

5

The Elephant as Servant

Many, many years ago, a wise man lived in a lonely house far away in the Himalaya Mountains. Next to the house stood a beautiful banyan tree, and on warm, sunny days the wise man liked to sit in the shade of its branches and think. One afternoon he looked up and saw a great flock of elephants flying toward him (for in those long-ago imaginary days all elephants could fly). The tired elephants were looking for a place to rest, and seeing the tree, they immediately swooped down and sat on it. But the beasts were so heavy that the branches broke. Soon the beautiful tree was nothing but a pile of sticks. "Oh, you miserable animals!" screamed the wise man. "You have ruined my tree! Let this be your punishment. You shall never fly again. From this day on elephants shall be ridden by man." And that, according to the people of India, is how the elephant became man's servant.

In Asia, elephants have been working for man for a long time, but no one knew exactly how long until archaeologists discovered a mysterious mound of earth at Mohenjo-daro in Pakistan. They began to dig, and it was not long before they found a great forgotten city, 4,000 years old. It was quite a place. The narrow streets were lined with shops, restaurants, and two-story brick houses. Excavators explored the ruins of a fort, a granary, and a bathhouse and found hundreds of little stone seals with words and pictures carved on them. No one has been able to figure out what the words mean, but the pictures speak for themselves. They tell their own story of what life was like in that city so very long ago.

Some of the seals are decorated with pictures of elephants. Archaeologists find these particularly fascinating, because the animals seem to have cloths or saddles on their backs. No one has ever seen a wild elephant wearing clothes, so the animals shown in these pictures must have been tame. Evidently, elephants had been caught and trained by the people of Mohenjo-daro 4,000 years ago.

Of course, we don't know exactly how they captured elephants then, but it is possible that their methods were very much like the ones used today. In Asia, catching these valuable animals has always been a job for professionals, and in some places families specialize in the work. A father teaches his son the trade, which the son will teach his son one day, and so on. Some families have been catching elephants for generations.

There are all sorts of different ways to capture an elephant alive. Some trappers mix drugs with food they know the animals like and leave the drugged "treat" in a place that no elephant could miss. If the animal is foolish enough to eat the food, the drug makes it drowsy, and the trapper can easily capture the groggy beast. But elephants aren't usually fooled. They don't like the smell of humans and know after a few sniffs that the food has been tampered with. Drugged food will probably work only with a very hungry elephant—or a very greedy one.

Other kinds of bait seem to be more successful. For instance, if a trapper wants to catch a bull, the very best bait is a tame female elephant.

Once he has taken the tame cow into the forest, the trapper leaves her alone and hides. If he is lucky, a wild male elephant will see her, find her interesting, and come over to introduce himself. While the male is busy courting the charming female, the trapper ropes and captures him.

For further excitement, men also catch elephants with a lasso. For this they need at least five men and three tame elephants. Each of the tame elephants must play a special part: It will be either a fighter, a beater, or a captor. The fighter elephants carry one man; all the others carry two.

First the beater chases a wild elephant through the forest until it is exhausted. Then the captor elephant, carrying the hunter and his assistant, moves close to the wild animal. The hunter holds a twenty-five-yard lasso made of buffalo hide in his hands. The wild elephant tries to escape, but the man is too quick. The long rope whizzes through the air. An instant later the lasso is tightly looped around one of the elephant's hind feet. The hunter's assistant slides to the ground and quickly ties the other end of the rope to a tree. The furious animal tries to attack, but the fighter elephant charges in and battles with it while the hunters move to a safe place. After a while, the captured animal realizes it cannot escape. The struggling stops, and soon the tame elephants lead it to a training camp.

The very best way to capture elephants, however, is the *keddah.* A keddah is an enormous corral. Inside there is a pond or stream and plenty of trees and bushes. Around the outside is a deep ditch and a stockade of large strong logs. The gate to the stockade can be raised and lowered, and wooden platforms are built just outside the corral.

When the keddah is ready, a large number of men (called beaters) surround a herd of elephants and begin to make noise. The elephants try to move away from the racket, but the beaters follow, pushing them slowly toward the corral. When the elephants are close to the gate, the men quickly put up a bamboo fence around them. The beaters keep making noise while they wait for a signal from their chief. When he decides the time is right, one man hides by the gate, and several others climb onto the platforms. The beaters start pushing the elephants toward the entrance. When they are almost at the gate, there is an explosion of noise. Men scream, shake rattles, and fire guns. The elephants panic and run in the only direction they can—straight through the gate. The gate falls behind them, and they are prisoners.

After this the animals are sorted out. Trainers ride into the corral to choose the animals they want. Old, sick, or injured elephants are usually set free.

The keddah is an excellent way to capture elephants, but it

does present two problems. The first is that you may accidently capture a lot of animals you don't want. The second is that it takes almost a thousand men to make it work.

Once an elephant has been caught, its training begins. This is a difficult job, and to do it well a man must have great courage and patience. In India an elephant trainer is called a *mahout*. In Burma trainers are known as *oozies*.

Oozies start to learn about elephants when they are little boys. A six-year-old must know how to sit on an elephant. A fourteen-year-old will already be working as an oozie's assistant. An oozie must love elephants because he will spend endless hours working with them.

In the Burmese teak forests, oozies get up before dawn to catch their elephants, for at night the animals are allowed to roam through the woods while they eat. In the morning an oozie may have to track his elephant through eight miles of thick jungle. To do this, he must be able to recognize footprints and the sound of his elephant's voice. On the way he checks the animal's droppings to find out what it has been eating. Like human beings, elephants must have a balanced diet. Has his elephant been eating too much bamboo? Too much grass?

He catches the elephant, rides it to camp, and gives it a bath. He scrubs it, rinses it, and polishes its tusks. Finally the elephant is harnessed and ready for work.

Oozie and elephant work together until three o'clock. Then the oozie takes off the harness and puts on a special chain that keeps the elephant from wandering too far during the night. The elephant goes off to eat, and the oozie checks the harness and equipment. If any of the straps or buckles are broken, he repairs them. Only after all that is done can he relax and forget about elephants.

Generally, an elephant makes friends with only one human being at a time, and that particular person is the only one the animal will obey. A trained elephant loves and obeys its oozie. In return, the oozie loves the animal, teaches it, and takes great pride in its accomplishments. Oozie and elephant are often very much like parent and child.

Elephants are not trained overnight. It is a long, painful business, and there are many different ways to go about it.

In Cambodia, 600 years ago, newly captured elephants were tied up, left without food, and tormented by a masked man dressed in black. The masked man screamed at the elephant and beat it so cruelly that the creature soon learned to hate and fear its horrible visitor. Then, after seven days of this treatment, a man without a mask suddenly appeared. He pretended to fight the masked man and to give the elephant's old enemy a terrible beating. The new trainer stayed with the elephant; he spoke gently, scratched the animal, and gave it food. As soon as the elephant learned to trust its kind new friend, the trainer tied the wild animal to a tame one and kept them together for twenty days. After that, the elephant could be taught to do anything.

In India today, a mahout generally chooses the animal he wants to train. With his assistants, he looks over the animals in the keddah. The youngest elephants are easiest to teach, but very young animals can't do heavy work. The mahout will probably pick a fifteen- or twenty-year-old.

The mahout and his assistant mount a tame elephant and ride into the corral. They single out the animal. Quickly the assistant slips to the ground. Like a cowboy roping a calf, he loops one end of his rope around the elephant's back foot. The other end is tied to the tame animal, which leads the wild elephant out of the corral.

Outside they tie the animal to a very strong tree—the stronger the better, because when the elephant realizes what has happened, it has an elephant-size tantrum. It kicks, screams, struggles, and refuses to eat—but still it remains a prisoner. The days pass. Finally, the miserable, tired, hungry creature knows it cannot win. It calms down, starts to eat, and is soon taken to a training camp.

The elephant is trained by a mahout and two assistants. At the first lesson, the mahout stands in front of the animal. In his hand he holds a *hawkus,* a stick with a sharp metal point. The assistants, riding on tame elephants, position themselves on either side. To calm the wild animal, they sing a soothing lullaby, but the elephant isn't interested. Using its trunk like a giant club, it tries to attack the mahout—and gets a very painful surprise. Each time the elephant swings at the mahout, the mahout pricks its trunk with his hawkus. After several days of this, the trunk becomes very sore. The elephant has been punished enough. It stops trying to hurt the mahout. It has learned its first and most important lesson.

After several weeks, the mahout tries to ride the elephant for the first time. Most elephants don't like that at all and often act like bucking broncos. Like a rodeo cowboy, the mahout must somehow manage to stay on.

Gradually, the elephant learns to obey certain signals. By using his feet to kick or squeeze the animal behind the ears, a rider can tell the elephant to go forward or backward, to kneel down or stand up.

Elephants can also learn to obey thirty different word commands. A well-educated twenty-five-year-old lumber elephant knows twenty-five different word commands and can pick up a knife, ax, chain, or stick.

Most lumber elephants are born in captivity, which means they are much easier to train. In Burma, five-year-old calves are taken to a camp where a special pen, called a *crush,* has been built.

While the mother elephant watches, trainers coax the calf into the pen with a banana. Then one of the trainers puts on a harness that is attached to a very long rope. The man with the harness stands on a high platform. His assistants hold the rope and lower him slowly down until he is sitting on the calf's back. The calf thrashes and bellows. When this happens, the rider is pulled up into the air and off the calf's back. As soon as the animal calms down, the rider is lowered again—and again and again—until the fussing stops and the man is able to ride the calf.

After this, the trainers start work with another rope. This rope has a padded block of wood at the end. The block is lowered until it touches the elephant's back. At first, the calf bucks. But after several tries, the calf sits down when the block is lowered. When this happens, all the trainers yell, "*Hmit!*"—"Sit." When the block is raised, the calf stands, and the trainers shout, "*Tah!*"—"Get up." After a day of this, a rider can sit on the elephant and order it to sit or stand.

These training sessions are long, and the trainers sometimes get tired and frustrated, but no one is ever cruel to the animal. The elephant is always treated with great kindness and given lots of treats as rewards for good behavior.*

* Information from J. H. Williams, *Elephant Bill.*

Some trainers feel that elephants should be taught only with kindness. They never use a hawkus or punish the animal in any way. Others feel that a mixture of reward and punishment works best. All agree, however, that when you are training an elephant, you must never let it disobey a single command.

Once an elephant has learned the first simple lessons, it can be trained for all kinds of work.

In Asia, elephants have done the work of cars, trucks, and buses for centuries. A single man can sit on the elephant's neck and ride the animal quite easily. If several people want to travel, a wooden seat called a *howdah* is strapped to the elephant's back, and everyone climbs aboard. Riding in a howdah sounds like fun, but people who have tried it say that after a while the elephant's swaying walk may make them very seasick.

Although riding in a car is more comfortable, it is smarter to ride an elephant if you are planning to travel through the jungle or go tiger hunting. The animal is strong enough to plow through the thick brush, and tall enough to keep you out of the tiger's reach. A really well trained elephant may actually be able to spear a leaping tiger with its sharp, pointed tusks.

In the 4,000 thousand years that elephants have been working for man, they have done a great deal more than carry people from place to place. At one time, elephants hauled the great blocks of stone that were used to build palaces, walls, and temples. Elephant labor built the great mosque in the city of Samarkand, and elephants carried huge evergreen trees from distant forests to the emperor of China's garden. Elephants even played an important part in World War II. British soldiers used elephants to help build bridges, and Japanese soldiers loaded the animals with bundles and employed them as giant supply trucks.

Today, in Burma, elephants haul teak logs just as they have for centuries because modern machines cannot be used in those wild, remote forests.

Teak, an extremely tough, long-lasting, valuable wood, is usually used to make furniture, but 200 years ago it was used to build English ships.

England is a long way from Burma. It is a lonely little island sitting on the edge of Europe. It doesn't look very important, but once the English almost ruled the world. They dominated it with a fleet of wooden sailing ships—fighting ships and merchant ships—that made that little island into a rich, powerful nation.

The English needed their ships, and the shipbuilders needed wood to make them. The best wood came from oak trees, but there was never quite enough of it. Trees had to be 80 to 120 years old before they were big enough to be used, and it sometimes took 700 trees just to make a single vessel. Shipbuilders tried using other kinds of wood, but nothing worked until they discovered teak.

Teak was just as strong as oak, and at the end of the eighteenth century the English began to use this tough, sturdy wood. Oozies and elephants were hired to harvest the teak, and shipbuilders hammered the wood into dozens of English ships. Some of these ships sailed into battle and helped the English win the war against Napoleon. Others carried cargoes of ivory, silk, spice, tea, and tobacco that helped make the country rich. Hundreds of English sailors who had never seen an elephant walked the decks of ships that elephants had helped to build.

Although elephants are good workers, people who depend on elephant labor do have certain problems. For instance, elephants can pull great weights, but they aren't very good at carrying things. An elephant can carry only one-tenth its own weight. This means that six ponies can do the work of one elephant, and one truck can do the work of several elephants. Elephants also get tired easily, and they cannot work long hours. In fact, the average elephant workday is only five hours long. They cannot work in hot weather, and they need so many vacations that in the teak forests they work about 150 days out of the entire year. Elephants are loyal servants, but machines are more practical. Machines don't have to be trained and cared for, and they don't get tired. In Asia times are changing. Each year the people use more machines and fewer elephants. It seems that after a 4,000-year career, the working elephant is about to go into retirement.

The Elephant as Warrior

Six hundred years ago, people in Central Asia spoke in frightened whispers of the "great gray wolf" who was eating the earth. It was not a real animal they feared, but a fierce warrior named Tamerlane. With his mighty armies, Tamerlane moved swiftly through southern Russia, Afghanistan, and Persia, conquering kingdoms, destroying cities, slaughtering all who stood against him. In no time at all, Tamerlane, the lame son of an unimportant Tartar chieftain, had made himself the ruler of a mighty empire.

But the empire wasn't big enough. Tamerlane wanted more, so in 1398 he decided to conquer India.

Tamerlane was cruel and greedy, but he wasn't stupid. Before beginning this enterprise, he commanded his best scholars to find out as much about India as they could. Their report was alarming. The Indians, it seemed, had a dreadful weapon: elephants. Swords and arrows bounced off their thick hides. They crushed men with their mighty trunks and tossed horses into the air as if they were pebbles. The mere sight of these awful beasts made brave men tremble. Tamerlane listened to the learned men, considered the problem carefully, and then asked the scholars where they would like to be during the battle. "With the ladies, please, sire," they replied.

Despite the grim reports, Tamerlane gathered his forces, marched to India, and camped outside the great walled city of Delhi.

Inside the city, Prince Mahmoud marshaled his army—10,000 horsemen, 40,000 foot soldiers, and a company of elephants in full battle array. The light glinted on the elephants' armour and on the poisoned daggers tied to their tusks. On their backs the animals carried huge wooden towers filled with soldiers armed with bows, arrows, rockets, and boiling tar. When Mahmoud gave the signal, the great brass drums thundered, the cymbals crashed, the trumpets screamed, and the great Indian army poured out through the city gates. The sight was so terrifying that every man in Tamerlane's army trembled. Even the great Tamerlane himself was so frightened that he fell on his knees to pray.

Perhaps his prayers were answered, because he managed to pull himself together and lead his army into battle. By the end of the day, he had conquered the city of Delhi, murdered most of its people, and captured some of those terrible elephants.

Tamerlane was certainly not the first general to be frightened by war elephants. No one knows exactly when the animals were used in battle for the first time, but by the time of Alexander the Great (366–323 B.C.) there were plenty of well-trained fighting elephants in Asia.

Alexander lived only thirty-three years. At twenty he became king of a small country north of Greece called Macedon. In the next thirteen years he made himself ruler of the world—master of Greece, Persia, Egypt, and India.

But before Alexander could conquer India, he had to defeat the army of King Porus. On the banks of the river Hydaspes, the Indian and Macedonian armies stood face to face. Alexander cast his eye over Porus's forces. Fifty thousand foot soldiers, 3,000 horsemen, 300 war chariots, and 200 elephants stretched like a glittering wall across the plain. Towering over the others and seated on the largest elephant was Porus, a giant of a man, some seven feet tall. Even Alexander was impressed. "At last," said he, "I have met a danger worthy of the greatness of my soul."

The battle began. The elephants advanced, crushing the Macedonians as they went. Alexander's men attacked with arrows and long spears. Both armies fought bravely, but little by little the tide began to turn in favor of Alexander.

Porus knew the battle was lost. He was exhausted and

wounded, but still he fought on, too proud to surrender. Finally, faint from loss of blood, he collapsed on the back of his elephant. The animal realized that Porus might fall, so it knelt and gently placed its master on the ground. Using its trunk with a surgeon's skill, it carefully pulled the spears and arrows from the Indian king's body.

Later, Porus was brought to Alexander as a prisoner. "How shall I treat you?" the Macedonian asked. "As a king," Porus replied. Alexander was so greatly moved by the man's courage and nobility that he set Porus free and gave him back his kingdom.

Legends say that even the elephant was rewarded for its bravery. The Macedonian king placed two gold rings on its tusks and declared that the animal was to be given the name of one of the greatest Greek heroes: Ajax.

In ancient times an elephant was as powerful and feared a weapon as a missile with a nuclear warhead is today. Generals depended on these animals, and it isn't hard to understand why. A group of elephants could trample an army or batter down the walls of a city. When sent into battle carrying a tower full of armed men, an elephant was the equivalent of a modern armed tank. Warrior elephants could inflict tremendous physical damage on the enemy, but that wasn't the most important reason for using them. When soldiers saw elephants for the first time, they were often so frightened that they forgot to fight; they simply dropped their weapons and ran. Horses panicked and refused to charge, and the elephants won easy victories. In the ancient world, elephants were such valuable weapons that every king wanted to have some, and a few rulers, like Queen Semiramis of Assyria, went to incredible lengths just to get hold of a few of these remarkable animals.

No one knows exactly when Queen Semiramis lived. In fact, the story of her life is such an amazing mixture of history and legend that it is hard to figure out where truth begins and fictions ends. Most of the information we have comes from the works of an ancient writer named Diodorus, who says that Semiramis, the daughter of a goddess, was a great queen, an excellent general, and an extremely beautiful and ambitious woman. Like Alexander and Tamerlane, she wanted to conquer India.

At that time, there were no elephants outside India. Semiramis knew that if she marched into battle with a company of elephants, she could scare the entire Indian army out of its wits. The only problem was recruiting the animals. Since there weren't any elephants in Assyria, Semiramis decided to make some.

She put hundreds of people to work. For days they snipped and stitched and sewed. When they were finished, Semiramis had an army of elephant puppets—made of ox hide stuffed with straw. Each of the puppets was mounted on a camel, and two men were assigned to ride on the "elephant's" back. The stuffed creatures looked very peculiar, but Semiramis was delighted. Since she had probably never seen an elephant, she thought the puppets looked exactly like the real thing.

Semiramis thought she was going to give the Indian king the surprise of his life, but a few Assyrian soldiers spoiled the plan. They secretly told the enemy all about the phony elephants. When Semiramis marched her puppets into battle, the Indian soldiers weren't frightened at all since they had been warned in advance. But there was no way to warn the horses. They were terrified by the sight of the strange monsters. The victory, however, belonged to the real elephants of the Indian army, which thundered in and trampled the dummies to bits.

At first all war elephants came from Asia, but it was difficult and expensive to ship them from there to Europe and North Africa. Eventually, King Ptolemy Philadelphius of Egypt thought of a solution. He sent out an expedition to capture a few of the wild African elephants that lived near Egypt. The idea was a success, and by 280 B.C. African elephants were being caught and trained for war. In fact, the most famous war elephants in history, the elephants of Carthage, were African animals.

In 264 B.C. there were two great competing powers. On one side of the Mediterranean Sea, on the coast of North Africa, stood the city of Carthage. On the other side was the city of Rome. Each wanted to be the greatest power; each wanted to control the Mediterranean. To decide which power would triumph, they fought three terrible wars, called the Punic Wars, which lasted from 264 B.C. to 146 B.C.

The greatest of all the generals to fight in these campaigns was a Carthaginian named Hannibal.

Hannibal was only nine years old when his father made him swear before the gods that he would always be the enemy of Rome. He kept his oath. During the Second Punic War, he even tried to conquer the city of Rome itself.

His plan was very clever. Look at the map. You can see that the shortest route from Carthage to Rome is straight across the Mediterranean. If Hannibal had attacked that way, the Romans would have been ready and waiting for him. Instead, he planned a surprise: He marched his army from North Africa to Spain, and from Spain to southern France. From there he planned to cross the Alps into Italy.

At first things went smoothly, but when Hannibal reached the banks of the Rhone River in France, his troubles began. The Rhone was a wide, deep, swift river, and Hannibal had to get 50,000 foot soldiers, 9,000 horsemen, mules, baggage, and 37 elephants safely across.

The elephants were the most serious problem. Although they are good swimmers, elephants often tire and drown when they have to swim a long way against a strong current. Hannibal knew his elephants would never be able to swim across the Rhone, so he put his men to work building giant rafts. The Carthaginian soldiers even covered the tops of the rafts with soil and grass so the elephants would feel at home. But when the time came to board the rafts, the creatures wouldn't budge. The trainers shouted and prodded, but it was no use. The elephants wouldn't move. Finally, after a great deal of coaxing, the trainers cleverly persuaded two females to step on board; the other elephants followed, and the rafts were launched.

Most of the elephants crossed safely, but a few realized they had been tricked. When they found themselves stuck on swaying rafts in the middle of a river, they panicked and jumped, right into the deep, icy water. The riders drowned, but the frightened elephants began to swim. Using their trunks as snorkels and paddling furiously, they crossed the river and climbed out on the opposite bank.

Hannibal had crossed the Rhone, but the Alps were still in front of him. It was November. The sky was gray and the wind cold; snowflakes drifted down from the sky, and the mountains looked

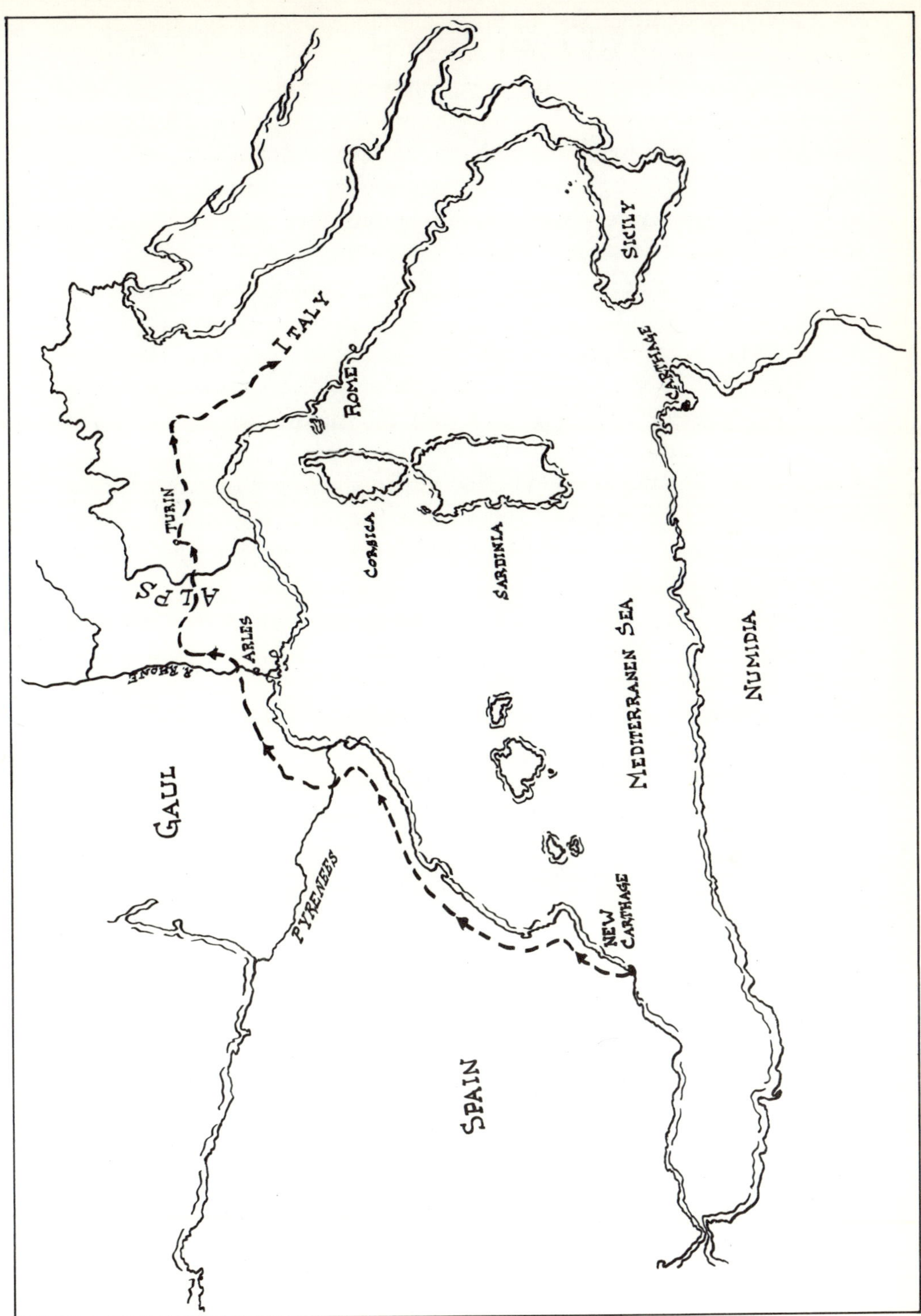

Hannibal's route across the Alps

David Tripp

dark and threatening. The frightened soldiers wanted to turn back, but Hannibal would not admit defeat. He called his men together, looked out over the shivering ranks, and said angrily, "Tell me why brave men are so afraid? You have climbed the Pyrenees Mountains, crossed the Rhone, and now suddenly, at the gates of Italy, you pause. What do you think the Alps are? They are no worse than any other mountains. Men have crossed them before. Are you unable to do what other men have done? Either you stop here and admit you are cowards, or you march forward like heroes until you reach the very walls of Rome!"

There was no further talk of turning back. When Hannibal gave the order to march, the Carthaginian soldiers picked up their gear and began the long, hard trek over the mountains.

The trails were difficult. The weather was freezing. Soldiers stumbled on the icy paths and tried not to slide over the treacherous cliffs. The tribesmen who lived in the mountains attacked. There was very little to eat. Men and animals shivered and starved, but Hannibal marched on.

On the way down, the Carthaginians were caught in a blinding snowstorm. The path was so slippery that the soldiers could barely stand. The animals, weighed down by their heavy bundles, became stuck in the snow. A landslide blocked the path, and a road had to be cleared.

After two terrible weeks, the army reached Italy. Half the men were dead, but all thirty-seven elephants arrived safely.

Soon there was work for the giant animals to do. In December, when the Roman and Carthaginian armies clashed beside the Trebia River, the elephants frightened the Roman horses so badly that Hannibal won a tremendous victory.

The Carthaginian general kept marching toward Rome, but it was a bitterly cold winter and the army was sick and hungry. A violent infection left Hannibal blind in one eye. Men and animals died. Soon there was only one elephant left: Surus, the bravest elephant and the only Asiatic animal in the army. When Hannibal became too sick even to ride his horse, his physicians wrapped him in blankets and mounted him on Surus's back. All through that long cold winter, the one-eyed general and his elephant led the tired, freezing army through Italy.

More elephants were finally sent from Carthage, and the war dragged on. The Romans were afraid of the animals, and Hannibal was willing to do almost anything to protect their fearsome reputation.

Pliny the Elder, a Roman soldier and naturalist, claimed that Hannibal once made all his Roman prisoners fight to the death. At the end of the battle, only one man was still alive. The Carthaginian commander promised this prisoner his freedom—on one condition: He had to fight an elephant and win. There wasn't much of a chance, but the Roman decided to try. The laughing soldiers crowded around to watch the battle, but soon the jeering stopped: The Roman was winning. Then, suddenly, there was silence. The Carthaginians were stunned. The prisoner had actually managed to kill the beast! Hannibal kept his promise and let the man go. But Carthaginian soldiers secretly murdered the unlucky Roman to prevent him from telling anyone that a man could defeat an elephant single-handedly.

Hannibal won victory after victory, but because the Carthaginian government refused to send the troops and supplies he needed, he never conquered the city of Rome. Eventually, the Romans sent an army to North Africa, and Hannibal had to rush home to defend the city of Carthage. The Second Punic War ended when the Roman general, Scipio, met Hannibal's army at Zama, on the dusty plains of North Africa.

For years the Romans had been beaten by elephants, but at Zama Scipio showed that they could learn from their mistakes. The Roman general based his battle plan on three important facts: untrained horses are frightened of elephants; charging elephants trample people underfoot; and all elephants, even trained ones, can be frightened by loud noises.

When he reached Zama, Scipio arranged his troops carefully, leaving wide spaces between the columns of soldiers so the charging elephants would not trample his men. He ordered his cavalrymen to dismount before the battle began. When the Carthaginian elephants charged, he ordered the Roman musicians to blow a tremendous blast on their trumpets. The elephants panicked. Hannibal was defeated, and Zama was a great Roman victory.

The Romans, however, were still worried about those elephants. Before the peace treaty could be signed, Carthage had to agree to give up its war elephants and promise not to train any more.

But the Carthaginians never forgot their elephants. H. H. Scullard, in his book *The Elephant in the Greek and Roman World,* says that years later, at the end of the Third Punic War, when the Roman armies were at the gates of Carthage and the desolate city was about to be destroyed, the Carthaginians wandered helplessly through the streets. Some wept; some prayed. Others shouted the names of their elephants—perhaps hoping for a miracle that would bring the mighty animals back to save them.

Elephants were powerful weapons, but not all generals used them. Alexander, for instance, captured a great many but never sent a single one into battle. The Romans were expert at elephant fighting but never really liked using the animals in their armies. Elephants were an excellent weapon, but they were also rather unpredictable, and in battle they were sometimes more of a nuisance than a help. A wound, a loud noise, a small animal, or the death of its trainer could scare an elephant out of its wits. The terrified animal would run wild, smashing and trampling both friends and enemies. Because there was no way to calm a raging, panic-stricken elephant, the mahout killed it instantly by hammering a chisel into the joint between the animal's head and neck. Unfortunately, frightened elephants were a common problem. In fact, at the battle of Metaurus in 207 B.C., mahouts killed more elephants than the enemy.

Actually, elephants were never meant to be warriors. They are peaceful creatures that fight only to defend themselves. Man had to teach the elephant to kill in cold blood—and it wasn't easy.

In Asia, hundreds of years ago, unlucky criminals were executed by being crushed under an elephant's foot. Although the animals were trained to do this unpleasant job, they were often unwilling. In a book about India called *Storia do Mogor,* Signor N. Manucci tells what happened at one of these executions.

The king of Ceylon sentenced a young prince to death and ordered one of the prince's own elephants to slay him. When the animal approached, the frightened victim cried out and begged the animal not to kill him. At the sound of the familiar voice, the elephant stopped and stubbornly refused to hurt its former master. The mahout shouted and threatened, but the elephant wouldn't move. Finally, the king leaped from his throne and ordered the elephant to carry out the sentence. The animal knew it had to obey a royal command. Closing its eyes, it rushed at the prince and killed him as quickly and mercifully as possible.

The men who trained war elephants had similar problems. They could teach elephants to obey orders, but they couldn't turn them into angry, hostile animals—and they certainly couldn't teach them to be enthusiastic about going into battle. Mahouts often coped with this problem by using large doses of wine and drugs to give their elephants a little fighting spirit.

Despite all these problems, war elephants were used until the time came when battles were fought with guns and cannon instead of bows and arrows. The sound of these noisy gunpowder weapons frightened the elephants so badly that they were absolutely useless in battle.

Elephants were the warriors and servants of the ancient world—so highly valued that Asian princes and kings passed laws to protect them. In Ceylon, 500 years ago, any man who killed an elephant was punished with a flogging, a fine, and imprisonment. But times have changed. Because machines have made elephants obsolete in industry and on the battlefield and the human population in India and Asia has risen to such alarming proportions, growing food is now considered far more important than preserving elephants. In India guns are now issued to farmers so they can protect their fields from intruding elephants. In Ceylon and Sumatra, farmers have guarded their crops so energetically that elephants have almost completely disappeared. Fortunately, there are still a great many people in Asia who do want to protect and preserve wildlife. They have established national parks, punished poachers, and tried to protect farmers and elephants from each other.

Plate XIX, part 7, *Indiae Orientalis,* John Theodore Bry, 1604. Courtesy Trustees of the National Library of Scotland

Capturing elephants in a keddah

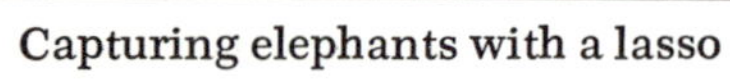

Capturing elephants with a lasso

From *An Account of an Embassy to the Kingdom of Ava in the year 1795,* Michael Symes, Constable, Edinburgh, 1827

From Un Hiver au Cambodge, Edgar Boulanger, Mame et Fils, Tours, 1887

Elephants carry members of a hunting expedition through the jungle.

Elephants in battle

Plate XVIII, part 7, *Indiae Orientalis*, John Theodore Bry, 1604. Courtesy Trustees of the National Library of Scotland

a. Elephants hauling lumber

b. Elephants in ceremonial dress with howdahs

c. An elephant and its trainer

d. Elephant executing a criminal

e. Hannibal crossing the Alps

a. From *The Ivory King,* Charles F. Holder, Scribner's, New York, 1886

b. From *The Ivory King,* Charles F. Holder, Scribner's, New York, 1886

c. From *Beast and Man in India,* John Lockwood Kipling, Macmillan, New York, 1892

d. From *The History and Romance of Crime fro Earliest Times to the Present Day,* Arthur Griffiths Grolier Society, n.d.

e. Cartoon by John Leech from *The Comic History c Rome,* Gilbert à Beckett, Bradbury Agnew, Londor 1890

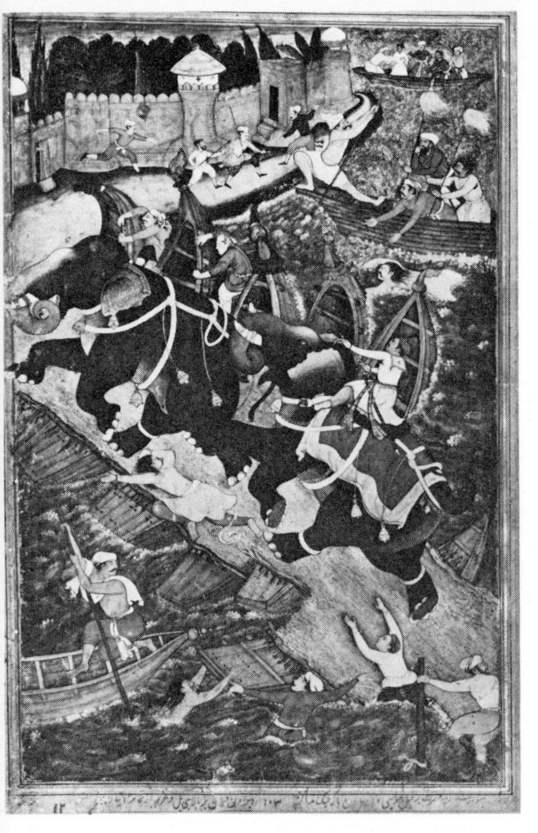

Courtesy Victoria and Albert Museum. Pages from the *Akbarnamah*, India, sixteenth century

Because elephants sometimes drowned while swimming, a bridge of boats was used to get the animals safely across the river.

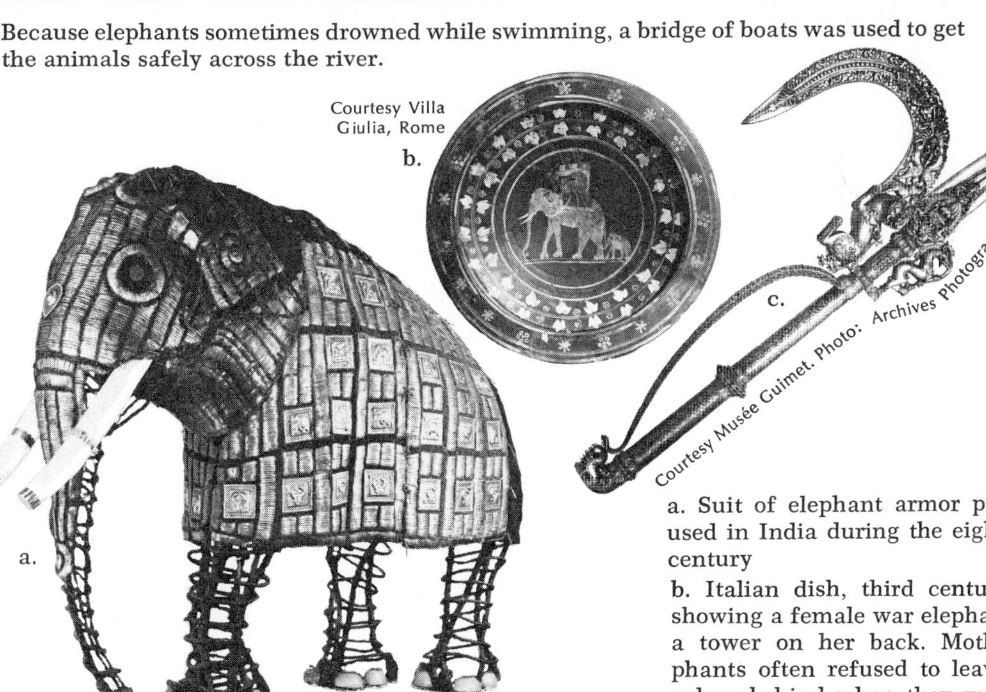

Courtesy Villa Giulia, Rome

Courtesy Musée Guimet. Photo: Archives Photographiques—Paris

ourtesy Tower of London Armouries, British Crown copyright—reproduced th permission of the Controller of Her Britannic Majesty's Stationery Office

a. Suit of elephant armor probably used in India during the eighteenth century

b. Italian dish, third century B.C., showing a female war elephant with a tower on her back. Mother elephants often refused to leave their calves behind when they went into battle.

c. Bronze hawkus used on ceremonial occasions. India, seventeenth century

7

The Elephant as Performer

Ladies and Gentlemen, I give you JUMBO:

"The ONLY MASTODON on EARTH
Whose Like the World will never See Again,
The Towering Monarch of His Mighty Race,
The GENTLE and HISTORIC LORD of BEASTS
The Prodigious Pet of both England and America . . ."*

And that was the way the American people were introduced to Jumbo, the most famous circus elephant of all.

Jumbo began his career in the London Zoo. He was the first African elephant to be brought to England alive, and the largest elephant in captivity. For many years, Jumbo lived a quiet life. Children rode on his back, patted his trunk, and fed him buns. Then, in 1881, for no apparent reason, Jumbo began to get temperamental. He behaved so badly that he could no longer be trusted to give children rides. The zoo officials didn't want to kill him, but they were worried about keeping him in the zoo. While they were trying to make up their minds, an American offered to buy Jumbo.

Phineas Taylor Barnum, the founder of the Ringling Brothers,

* M. R. Werner, *Barnum,* p. 345.

Barnum and Bailey Circus, was always looking for new and marvelous attractions. Certain that thousands of people would buy tickets to see the largest elephant in captivity, he offered the zoo £2,000 for Jumbo. The zoo officials accepted immediately. But when they announced that Jumbo was going to America, the British were outraged. Jumbo was everyone's pet. How dare they sell him! Newspapers printed drawings of a weeping elephant leaving home. Thousands of letters poured into newspaper offices. Finally, the editor of the *Daily Telegraph,* one of London's largest papers, decided to do something about it. He sent Barnum a telegram:

> "ALL BRITISH CHILDREN DISTRESSED AT ELEPHANT'S DEPARTURE. HUNDREDS OF CORRESPONDENTS BEG US TO INQUIRE ON WHAT TERMS YOU WILL KINDLY RETURN JUMBO."*

Barnum answered that he wouldn't give up Jumbo for a hundred thousand pounds. Jumbo had to go.

Overnight, Jumbo became the world's most famous elephant. Restaurants served "Jumbo stew" and "Jumbo ice cream." Shops sold "Jumbo perfume" and "Jumbo earrings." People even sang a song called, "Why Part with Jumbo the Pet of the Zoo?"

In the midst of all this, Barnum's agents were trying to bring the elephant to America. They found a ship big enough to carry him and had a special cage built. Then they tried to get him out of the zoo.

It seemed that Jumbo didn't want to leave. After one look at the new cage, he lay down and refused to have anything to do with it. All the coaxing and pleading in the world did no good. Jumbo wouldn't move.

The ship was ready to sail. Barnum's agents were frantic. They telegraphed America: "What shall we do?" "Let him lie there as long as he wants to. The publicity is worth it,"** Barnum replied.

The ship sailed, but Jumbo was still in the London Zoo. Barnum's agents bought the elephant another steamship ticket. Days passed. Weeks passed. After a month of waiting, Jumbo finally walked into the cage. Barnum's men sighed with relief. At last the

*Richard Carrington, *Elephants,* p. 211.
**M. R. Werner, *Barnum,* p. 341.

elephant was ready to go. Huge crowds of people came to say goodbye. Some even sent presents. One lady treated him to a drink of beer; another gave him a box of buns. A nobleman sent oysters and champagne.

Everything was ready—everything but Jumbo. As the horses were pulling his cage to the dock, he stuck his trunk through the bars, grabbed the horses' tails, and pulled! The horses bolted. They went galloping wildly through the streets, while the driver pulled the reins, shouted, and prayed. It seemed that horses, elephant, and man were all going to end up in the nearest ditch, but the driver got the runaways under control, and they all arrived safely at the dock. On March 25, 1882, Jumbo sailed for America.

When the ship arrived in New York, hundreds of people turned out to give Jumbo a hero's welcome. Men, women, and children leaned out of windows and crowded into the streets to see Jumbo march up Broadway with his trunk wrapped tightly around his keeper's hand.

Jumbo was just as popular in America as he had been in England. He traveled around the country in a magnificent red and gold boxcar called Jumbo's Palace Car, and people everywhere greeted him with shouts and applause. Americans were soon using a new word: "Jumbo." In shops, ladies and gentlemen no longer asked for the *extra large size;* they asked for the *jumbo* size instead.

Unfortunately, Jumbo's circus career came to a sudden end on September 13, 1885. Late that night, after the last performance of the circus, Jumbo and his trainer were walking back to the boxcar. They were crossing the railroad tracks when a freight train came thundering down the rails. By the time the engineer saw the elephant, it was too late. He slammed on the brakes, but there was no way to stop the speeding train. Moments later there was a terrible crash. Jumbo gave one great howl when the engine struck him, and a few minutes later he was dead.

The death of the great elephant saddened people all over the world. He had truly been, as a reporter for the *St. Thomas Daily Times* said, "the pet of thousands and friend of all."* There would never be another circus elephant quite like Jumbo. Barnum gave his skeleton to the American Museum of Natural History so that visitors

* James Bannerman, "The Tragical Death of the Great Jumbo," p. 29.

could still see one of the most famous and beloved elephants of all time.

Jumbo was probably the most famous circus elephant, but he was certainly not the first. Elephants have been circus performers for thousands of years.

Almost 2,000 years ago, the poet Juvenal said that there were only two things necessary to keep the people of Rome happy: bread and circuses. He was right. The Romans loved shows, and huge crowds came to see thrilling, death-defying acts performed in the arena. But instead of watching jugglers and trapeze acts, they came to see men and animals fight to the death. Professional fighters, prisoners of war, lions, tigers, bears, leopards, and elephants died to entertain these audiences. The more unusual the animal, and the more ferocious the fight, the better the people liked it.

Politicians who wanted to be popular often presented circuses, and after a while the spoiled citizens of Rome expected a man to pay for a circus whenever he got a new government job. Each man tried to outdo the others and present the most thrilling, amazing, spectacular show ever seen.

In 55 B.C. a Roman general named Pompey gave a tremendous show. Six hundred lions were slaughtered in the arena, and the high point of the spectacle was a battle between African men armed with spears and eighteen elephants.

The elephants fought bravely. One, so badly wounded that it could no longer stand, fought on its knees, snatching men's shields and hurling them into the air. But the men were tough, experienced fighters, and soon the elephants realized they were doomed. In their terror, they tried to break through the iron fence that kept them in the arena. But when they found there was no escape, the poor elephants began to moan and wave their trunks. The wretched creatures looked so pitiful that even the bloodthirsty Romans felt sorry for them. Some people in the crowd began to cry. Others got angry. Whose fault was it that those elephants were so miserable? Pompey's, of course. Suddenly a storm of shouting shook the stadium. People were on their feet, screaming and cursing Pompey and calling him names. The general must have felt this was a little unfair—after all, he was paying the bill for all this entertainment—but he didn't want to have a riot on his hands. He quieted the crowd by ordering the Africans to spare the elephants—and the entire audience watched the animals march proudly out of the arena. Those elephants were probably the only animals ever to move a Roman audience to pity.

The Romans, of course, weren't the only people who enjoyed these brutal spectacles. In Asia, lions, leopards, tigers, and elephants were made to fight for the public's amusement. These fights were as popular as football games are today. Even the Emperor Akbar of India (1542–1605), who couldn't bear the idea of killing animals for meat, enjoyed watching animal fights.

People liked watching elephant battles, but staging them was a problem because elephants almost never fight each other. Trainers generally got around this difficulty by using elephants on musth. If all the elephants were calm, then mahouts fed them a type of liquor called *arrack,* which made the animals run wild with rage.

In ancient times, elephants also participated in other kinds of entertainment. Roman audiences loved to watch animals doing tricks, and there were schools in Rome for training elephants. The graduates of these schools were amazing creatures that could dance, throw darts with their trunks, and even walk on tightropes. In fact, one of these trained elephants is actually supposed to have walked down a rope that stretched from the top of a theater balcony to the stage. It's a little hard to imagine an elephant on a tightrope, but Seneca and Pliny, two famous Roman writers, described such performances, so we assume they must have really happened.

Some of these elephants were also trained to be clowns, and Roman audiences crowded into the theaters to watch their stunts. At one famous performance, twelve elephants dressed in gorgeous togas pretended to be guests at an elegant dinner. They pranced onto the stage, seated themselves gracefully, and ate their food with the utmost delicacy. But in the middle of this extremely genteel party, one of the elephants filled his trunk with water and squirted his companions. A wild water fight followed, and by the end of the act, the elephants were soaking and the audience was wet and howling with laughter.

When elephants weren't performing in theaters, the Romans used them in parades. There were a lot of parades in Rome because Roman armies were often victorious, and whenever a general won a great victory, he was allowed to march through the city in a great triumphal procession. Sometimes, as a special mark of distinction, a very famous general was allowed to ride through the streets in a chariot drawn by four elephants. It was a terrific idea, but driving four elephants did pose some problems. Pompey, who never had much luck with elephants, once planned to drive one of these chariots in a victory parade. The elephants were harnessed, and the chariot was ready. Pompey climbed into the chariot; the elephants started forward, then suddenly stopped. The four animals couldn't squeeze through the narrow city gates, and the furious general had to switch chariots at the last minute.

Today, of course, it is difficult to imagine a circus without elephants. The show simply wouldn't be the same without elephants dancing in the ring, riding bicycles, rolling balls, and parading around the arena. Only the most intelligent elephants become performers. They learn their tricks well and seem to like showing off. During the show, these hard-working animals perform in the ring, but after the audience has gone home, they go to work backstage—hauling circus wagons, pulling tent ropes, and carrying boxes. If there is a fire, these intelligent animals can even be trusted to help handle the water hoses.

Actually, elephants don't have to do tricks to get attention; they are interesting just the way they are. People love to watch elephants behaving naturally, and zoo elephants have been attracting crowds since a king of Assyria put elephants in his private zoo almost 3,000 years ago. In ancient times there were zoos in Egypt and China, but the most famous zoo was in the city of Carthage. When the Carthaginian war elephants weren't fighting, they lived in a public park where people visited them regularly and children probably brought them onions and turnips to eat.

Until about 100 years ago, there were very few elephants in Europe, and most of these animals belonged to kings or very rich men. In the eighth century the caliph of Baghdad gave an elephant to Emperor Charlemagne of France. The present was an excellent choice: Charlemagne liked the animal so much that he took it along when he went traveling. When the creature died, the king had a huge drinking cup made from its tusks.

King Henry III of England also owned an elephant, but his was rather a problem. It was so big that there was no place to put it. In 1256 the king finally had to order the sheriff of London to build a special house for this unusual pet.

Some of the elephants that belonged to kings actually lived like kings. King Louis XIV of France owned an elephant that lived at the luxurious palace at Versailles and thoroughly enjoyed French cooking. Instead of eating hay and oats, the animal dined on eighty pounds of crusty French bread, several pails of well-seasoned soup, and twelve pints of wine each day.

There is no question about it: Elephants are one of the greatest public attractions of all time. Kings and princes, ladies and gentlemen, and children of all ages have crowded into zoos, theaters, and circus tents to see these fantastic animals. When a showman brought an elephant to Dublin in 1681, a mob of curious people swarmed around the animal's tent. Everyone wanted to get in, and some felt they had missed the chance of a lifetime because they were too poor to buy tickets. As things turned out, the elephant was the unluckiest of all. A fire broke out, and he was burned to death. Even after the accident, crowds of people could still be found at the circus grounds, poking through the ashes, hoping to find a bit of tusk or bone to take away as a souvenir of the strange, marvelous beast that still eluded them.

Elephants have been stars for over 2,000 years—headliners in zoos, circuses, movies, and plays. Machines have taken the place of elephant workers, and tanks have taken the place of elephant warriors, but nothing can ever replace the world's largest, greatest, and most magnificent performers.

8

The Elephant as God

Large, powerful, and intelligent, the elephant is respected by all living creatures, including man. In many parts of Africa, the elephant is the emblem of a mighty chief; and in Nigeria, members of the Hausa tribe think it is a great compliment to call a man *giwa*, which means "elephant." In Asia, people impressed by the size, strength, and wisdom of these animals have long believed that elephants are gods or holy spirits. In fact, one of the greatest and best-loved of all the Hindu gods of India is Ganesa, the god with the elephant's head.

Actually, Ganesa didn't always have an elephant's head. At birth, he looked like a normal child; and his proud mother, the goddess Parvati, invited all the gods and goddesses to admire her son. All of them came—all but the god Shani. Parvati's feelings were hurt, and she insisted on knowing why Shani had not accepted her invitation. The others explained that Shani had stayed away because of his terrible power: He could kill with a single glance and was afraid of injuring the baby. "Nonsense," said Parvati, and she made such a fuss that the reluctant Shani finally came. He looked down at the infant, and the thing he feared most happened. The child's head instantly turned to a smoldering heap of ashes. Parvati burst into tears, and the other gods and goddesses sent the unhappy Shani to find a new head for the baby. The god searched the world over and finally found what he was looking for—a sleeping elephant. In a flash, Shani cut off his head, carried it back, and gently placed the head of the wisest of all living creatures on the shoulders of Ganesa, the young god.

Ganesa is a great and good spirit, the god of wisdom, learning, and the arts. Hindu poets begin their books with a prayer to Ganesa; and in Bengal, a particularly bright schoolboy is sometimes honored with the nickname *Gonesh,* which is another way of pronouncing Ganesa. The elephant-headed god is also in charge of bringing good fortune. At exam time, when they need luck most, children bring candy, cakes, and cookies to Ganesa's shrines. They know that Ganesa, like all elephants, loves sweets, and the children hope that in return for the presents the god will bring them high marks. Travelers pray to Ganesa before beginning a journey, and businessmen pray to him before making a deal. In India, people believe that if a man says the twelve names of Ganesa at dawn, noon, and sunset, he will have good fortune, knowledge, and wealth.

Ganesa is not the only elephant to live among the Hindu gods. Indra, the powerful god of the heavens who brings rain and hurls thunderbolts, rides a great white, four-tusked elephant named Airavata. Together they rush through the air bringing storms, and when great masses of rain clouds gather and darken the sky, it is easy to imagine that the clouds aren't clouds at all but a mighty elephant galloping through the air. Some people even say that Airavata's trunk is actually a giant waterspout for pouring water on the thirsty earth.

In Asia, elephants have long been worshiped as gods, but in other parts of the world people believe that elephants are sometimes chosen to serve gods in special ways. One of the most important missions an elephant ever performed is described in the Koran, the sacred book of Islam.

In the year 571 a child named Muhammad was born in the city of Mecca. Muhammad was no ordinary child; he had a great destiny and would one day be known as a great prophet and the founder of the Islamic religion.

But it happened that in the same year that Muhammad was born, King Abraha of Yemen decided to conquer Mecca. Riding on the back of a huge elephant, Abraha himself led a mighty company of soldiers and war elephants toward the city. They had almost reached the city walls when Abraha's elephant suddenly stopped and knelt in the dust. The other elephants followed suit, and the entire army came to a dead stop. The king and his officers tried to coax the elephants forward, but they wouldn't budge. The men shouted and kicked and swore, but the elephants refused to move. The soldiers in the ranks began to whisper. Some said they wouldn't march on Mecca without the elephants. Finally, the desperate king tried to trick his elephant. He ordered it to turn away from Mecca, and the elephant obligingly stood up; but when Abraha tried to turn him toward the city, the animal refused to obey. At that moment a great flock of birds came flying across the sky. Each of these birds carried rocks in its claws, and as they glided past, they bombarded the army with the stones. The slaughter was terrible. Of all his men, Abraha alone survived to tell the tale of how God had commanded the elephants to save Mecca and the life of the Prophet Muhammad.

Other people thought that elephants were the only animals able to worship the gods. The ancient Greeks and Romans, for example, believed that elephants paid homage to the gods of the heavens. When the new moon appeared, they thought that elephants plucked leafy branches and waved them toward the sky in honor of the moon goddess. And when the shining sun rose in the east at dawn, they believed that the elephants respectfully lifted their trunks in prayer.

A sixth-century historian named John of Ephesus thought that some elephants were Christians, and in his book he told the story of an especially devout group of animals that lived in Constantinople. It seems that God had once helped these elephants to triumph over their enemies, so each time they passed a church, they stopped to give thanks. At a signal from the chief elephant, all the creatures bowed, prayed, and made the sign of the cross with their trunks.

Elephants, the friends and servants of the gods, were also supposed to possess magical powers. In India during the Middle Ages, people thought a person could predict the future by looking at an elephant. If the king's elephant had a spotted trunk, it meant the king was going to die. If the elephant had a narrow left cheek, the king was going to quarrel with his ministers. If the elephant had a narrow right cheek, the king was going to quarrel with his sons.

In Europe, elephant medicines once provided magic cures for all sorts of diseases. Elephant's blood was considered a great remedy for leprosy, a deadly skin disease, and the touch of an elephant's trunk was practically guaranteed to make a headache disappear. In ancient times, people even used elephant fat as a magic salve. They believed that if they rubbed it on their bodies before walking through a forest, they would have nothing to fear. No lion, tiger, bear, or wolf would dare attack.

Elephants have played a part in the religious beliefs of people all over the world. Hindus, Buddhists, Moslems, and Christians, the people of Africa, the ancient Greeks and Romans, modern Europeans and Americans have all admired the elephant for its size, its strength, its wisdom, and its ability to live in peace with all creatures. It is no wonder that the English poet John Donne in *The Progress of the Soul* called the elephant "nature's masterpiece" and the Bible declared that the elephant is "chief of the ways of God" (Job 40:19).

Royal MS 10 E IV f. 43v. Reproduced by permission of the British Library Board

◀ Elephants were taught to walk tightropes in ancient times, but the medieval artist who drew this picture had probably never seen a live elephant.

Zoo at Versailles during the reign of King Louis XIV. See elephant compound at right.
▼

Histoire des Ménageries de l'antiquité à nos jours, Gustave Loisel, Doin & Laurens, Paris, 1912

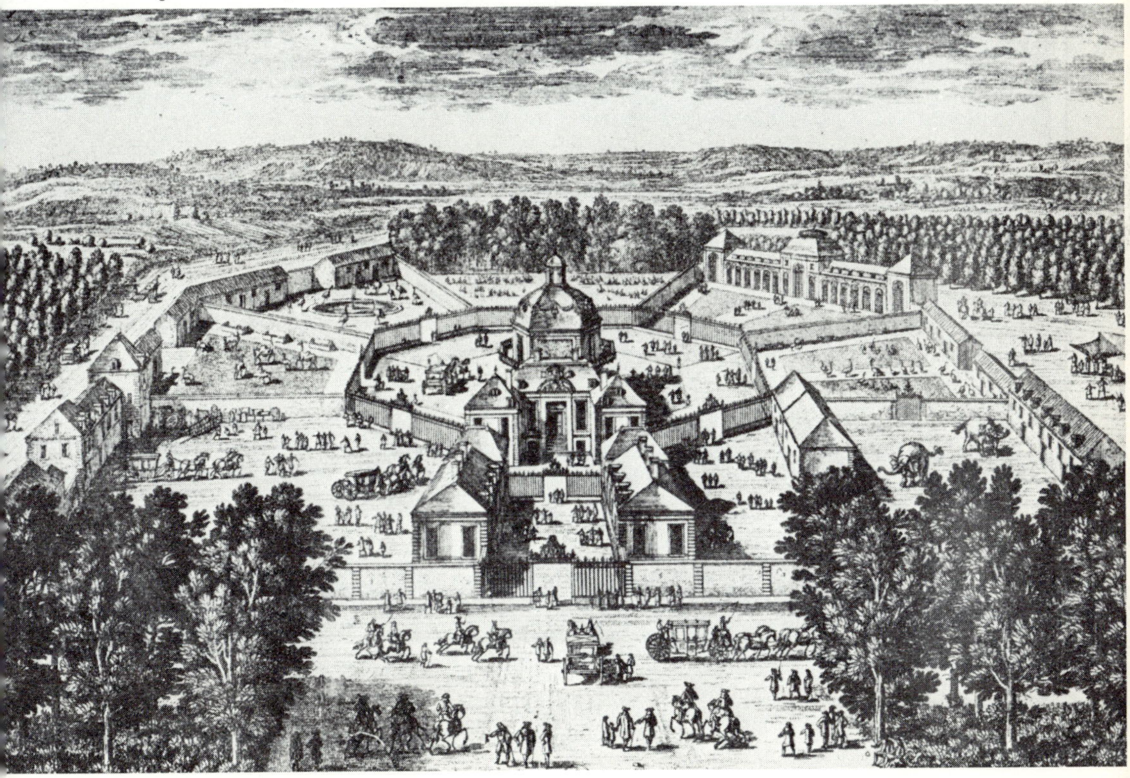

TOO WHITE FOR BARNUM
FOREPAUGHS REPLY TO BARNUM.
FOREPAUGH'S
SACRED WHITE ELEPHANT
"LIGHT OF ASIA"
PROVED BY THE HIGHEST SCIENTIFIC AUTHORITY TO BE
GENUINE
AND BARNUMS "SACRED WHITE?" ELEPHANT
AND ALL ITS SURROUNDINGS A RANK FRAUD.
Press of The Courier Company, Buffalo, N. Y.

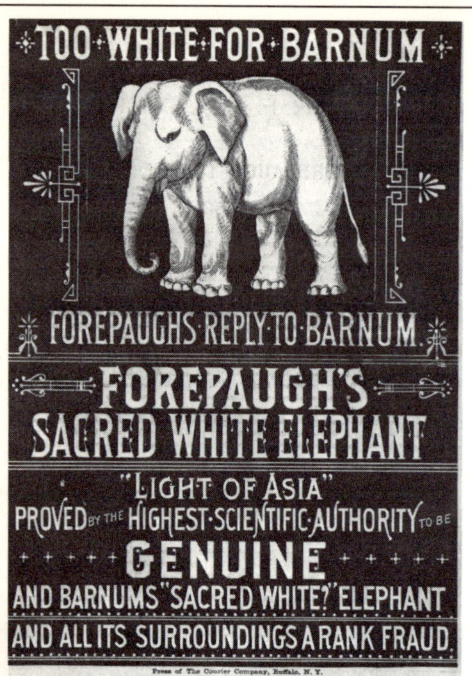

Courtesy McCaddon Collection, Princeton University Library

◀ Cover of a booklet advertising Forepaugh's phony white elephant

A slightly exaggerated poster showing the famous Jumbo giving rides to children at the London Zoo
▼

Courtesy Mr. and Mrs. Philip Sills

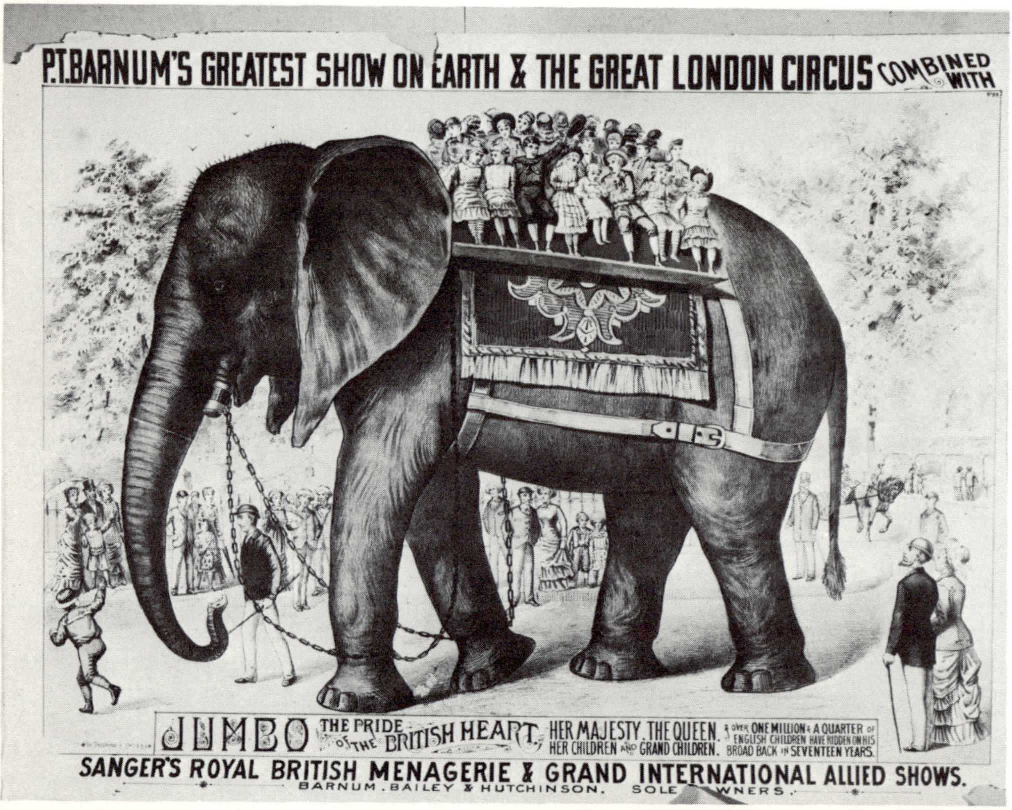
P.T. BARNUM'S GREATEST SHOW ON EARTH & THE GREAT LONDON CIRCUS COMBINED WITH
JUMBO
THE PRIDE OF THE BRITISH HEART.
HER MAJESTY, THE QUEEN, HER CHILDREN AND GRAND CHILDREN.
& OVER ONE MILLION & A QUARTER OF ENGLISH CHILDREN HAVE RIDDEN ON HIS BROAD BACK IN SEVENTEEN YEARS.
SANGER'S ROYAL BRITISH MENAGERIE & GRAND INTERNATIONAL ALLIED SHOWS.
BARNUM, BAILEY & HUTCHINSON. SOLE WNERS.

Courtesy Library of Congress

A very exaggerated poster. However, elephants enjoy performing, and they have learned to do all sorts of spectacular tricks.

Cartoon by Thomas Nast from *Harper's Weekly*, August 23, 1879

The elephant has had a place in American politics since cartoonist Thomas Nast first used it as a symbol for the Republican party one hundred years ago.

A perfect example of Barnum's advertising. Tom Thumb was present when Jumbo died, but Jumbo did not try to save the other elephant's life.

▼

WHO BACKED DOWN?

Courtesy Theatre Collection, The New York Public Library at Lincoln Center, Astor, Lenox and Tilden Foundations

Collection Vickie Carolyn Elson. Photo: Robert Woolard

Indian wall-hanging showing the Hindu god Ganesa

Photo: Susan Einstein

Courtesy Museum of Cultural History, UCLA

Fly whisk made of elephant hair

Drawing showing Indra, his queen, and his elephant, Airavata, riding through the clouds. India, nineteenth century ▼

Courtesy Museum of Fine Arts, Boston

9

The White Elephant

The most famous sacred elephants dwell in the heavens, but there are also a certain number of holy white elephants that live on earth. These real white elephants are very rare. They are albinos—animals whose bodies do not contain the chemical that gives eyes, hair, and skin their color. By rights a white elephant ought to be a beautiful animal with pale, creamy skin, but nature played a dirty trick. Actually, these animals have reddish-brown skin with white spots, pink or yellow eyes, and reddish hair. They may not be very pretty, but the people of Asia believe that each white elephant has a great, almost godlike spirit. The wisest and most famous of all these sacred animals is said to have appeared 500 years before the birth of Christ.

At that time, a wealthy Indian prince and his wife lived in a splendid palace near the snowy Himalaya Mountains. The princess was about to have a child, and shortly before the baby was born, she dreamed a very strange dream. While she slept she saw a beautiful white elephant come down from the gold and silver mountains. It walked around the palace three times, magically entered the princess's body, and vanished. When she woke, the royal lady was astonished and a little frightened. The dream meant that the spirit of a holy white elephant had been given to her unborn child. Soon after this, she gave birth to a son, and they named the infant Gautama.

When he grew to be a man, Gautama saw that all men suffered the pains of age, sickness, and death. This suffering saddened him, and with all his heart Gautama longed to find a way to end it. He left his wife and their child. The wealthy prince became a poor wandering monk who searched, meditated, and prayed for an answer. Finally, he received a great revelation, and for the rest of his life Gautama traveled all over the world, preaching that men could achieve perfect happiness by forgetting worldly things and learning to love the truth and care for others.

Soon Gautama became known as *Buddha,* which means "the enlighted one," the one who has found the truth. Buddha and his followers carried their message to people all over Asia. Today, Buddhism is one of the world's great religions, and Gautama is as important to Buddhists as Jesus is to Christians.

Not every white elephant has a spirit as great as Gautama's, but all white elephants are supposed to be holy, and in Asia people make a great fuss over them. In 1926 a white elephant was sent to the king of Thailand in a train that was specially equipped with showers and fans for the animal's comfort. But even this extravagant gesture was nothing compared to the kind of treatment a white elephant received in Thailand 100 years ago.

Anna Leonowens, an English governess who lived in Thailand for many years, says that in those days if a man found a white elephant, he rushed to tell the king—and got the most uncomfortable reward in history: His mouth, ears, and nose were stuffed with gold. An expedition was sent to trap the animal, and the newly captured white elephant traveled down the river to the capital in a magnificent wooden barge that was roofed with woven flowers and carpeted with mats edged in gold.

Servants brought gold and silver plates heaped with the juiciest grass, the sweetest sugar cane, and the most delicately baked wheat cakes, and the elephant feasted. Singers and dancers performed for the animal's pleasure. Gleaming golden rings were placed on the elephant's tusks, and on its head the elephant wore a splendid gold crown. Golden chains were clasped about its neck, and over its shoulders, servants draped a richly embroidered silk robe.

In a stable as luxurious as a palace, the elephant held court, and the most important men in the kingdom came to pay their respects and consult the elephant about matters of state. The greatest noblemen in the land watched the way the animal moved and listened to the sounds it made. A strange grunt or burp was often enough to keep the king from signing an important treaty.

No one, not even the king himself, could ride a white elephant, for that animal was as great a lord as the king. He was the king of the elephants, "before whom many thousands of elephants must bow and fall on their knees."*

If a white elephant got sick, the greatest doctors in the land were called to its bedside. Unfortunately, there was often little that any physician could do. Many of these elephants were actually killed with kindness—they died of eating too much rich food that wasn't good for them.

In the United States there aren't very many white elephants, but there are a great many white elephant sales. If you go to one, you will probably find a splendid collection of moth-eaten mink coats, bent bicycles, ugly silver teapots, and broken merry-go-round horses. The "white elephants" at a white elephant sale are the expensive, useless things that no one wants. But why call an expensive piece of junk a white elephant?

According to one legend, it all started in Asia. Many, many years ago, the king of Thailand decided to punish an offending courtier in a very peculiar way. Instead of cutting off his head or sending him to the deepest dungeon, the king gave the man a sacred white elephant. The delighted, unsuspecting courtier babbled his thanks for the splendid gift and took the creature home.

First he built a magnificent stable. Then he bought gold and silver dishes, jewels, and richly embroidered robes. Servants, musicians, and dancing girls were hired to care for the animal, and hundreds of pounds of the finest food were delivered to the elephant every day. But when the courtier saw the bills for all this, he turned a sickly shade of green. The cost of keeping the animal was emptying his treasury. In no time as all, the courtier was a ruined man. The elephant lived like a king, but his owner could barely afford to buy a bowl of rice for dinner. The king of Thailand probably chuckled nastily as he saw the courtier getting poorer every day.

Others say that people started to call expensive, useless things

*Anon., *The Elephant Principally Viewed in Relation to Man,* p. 172.

white elephants when P. T. Barnum bought a real white elephant for his Greatest Show on Earth. In 1883, two of Barnum's agents were traveling in Burma. There, for the first time, they heard of the sacred white elephant. No one in America had ever seen one, and a mysterious, holy elephant was just the sort of sensation Barnum needed for his show. It was against the law to take white elephants out of Burma—but that didn't stop Barnum's men.

The two Americans did a little research and discovered that the ruler of Burma, King Theebaw, had a great many financial problems. Although he was enormously rich, the king was always deeply in debt. Since His Majesty spent money faster than he made it, his minister of finance was always trying to scrounge up a little more to tide the king over. Finally, the minister became desperate—the king wanted money, but there wasn't a penny left. That was when Barnum's agents offered to buy a white elephant for $75,000.

The minister was delighted to sell them the elephant, but he certainly couldn't help them get it out of the country. It would be very awkward if the king's minister was caught breaking the law. So Barnum's men put their heads together and thought of a plan.

One very dark night, a gentle white elephant named Toung Taloung was painted red and blue. Yards and yards of cloth were draped over her back, and in this ridiculous costume she was smuggled on board a steamboat. In March 1884, she arrived in New York.

Barnum, dancing with excitement, could hardly wait to see his prize. But the sight of Toung Taloung made his mouth drop. He had expected a *white* elephant, not a spotty reddish mess.

It was a big disappointment, but Barnum was a determined man. He printed posters, he put up signs, he collected statements from people who swore that Toung Taloung was the finest white elephant they had ever seen. P. T. Barnum was the greatest salesman in America. He could probably have sold water to fish, but he couldn't sell tickets to see Toung Taloung. Everyone thought the elephant was a fake. Finally, even Barnum gave up. He sent his useless $75,000 elephant off to live with the other circus animals and started on a new project.

The story would have ended there if a rival showman named Adam Forepaugh hadn't tried to take advantage of Barnum's bad luck. Forepaugh took an ordinary gray animal, painted it white, and put it in his show. He claimed it was a *real* white elephant and invited the prince of Thailand, who was traveling in America, to see this shameful fraud. One look was enough. The furious, horrified prince turned around and stalked out. For a while, Forepaugh boldly told people that the prince had approved, but the showman soon lost his nerve. Notices suddenly appeared announcing that Forepaugh's elephant had died. Barnum chuckled and noted in his autobiography, *Struggles and Triumphs,* that the animal was simply "un-dyed."*

* P. T. Barnum, *Struggles and Triumphs,* p. 772.

EPILOGUE

The Elephant as Memory

In his book *On the Characteristics of Animals,* the Roman writer Aelian tells a wonderful story about elephants.

It seems that the ancient gods loved these animals so dearly that they decided to give them a special gift. At the foot of the Atlas Mountains in North Africa, the gods created a beautiful forest home for aged elephants. There in comfort and peace, free from want and danger, the animals were allowed to live out their lives in perfect happiness.

But it happened that near the forest there lived a greedy king. He had castles and servants and chests of gold and precious jewels, but all that wealth did not satisfy him. He wanted more, and each time he rode by the forest and saw the elephants walking among the trees, their long white tusks gleaming in the sun, he longed to get his hands on that ivory. He thought about the ivory day and night, and finally he could stand it no more. He commanded a group of huntsmen to go into the forest, kill the elephants, and return with a wagonload of the precious tusks.

The hunters set off on their errand. But they had no sooner entered the forest than one man gave a sudden cry and fell to the ground—dead. The frightened hunters wanted to turn back, but they dared not disobey the king's commands, so they walked farther into the magical forest. When they had gone a little way, another man gasped and clapped his hands to his chest. The others rushed to his aid, but by the time they reached him, he too was dead. One after another, the hunters mysteriously perished. Soon there was only one man left. The terrified hunter raced out of the enchanted forest, ran back to the castle, and gasped out his horrible tale. Never again did the king long for ivory. Never again did he try to hunt in the forest. He had been warned: No man dared touch animals that were protected by the gods.

Unfortunately, real elephants are not protected by the gods, and real elephants don't have magical powers. Despite their size and strength, elephants are helpless victims of the ivory merchant's greed, the spread of civilization, and the farmer's needs. Even in the great national parks, elephants aren't secure. In those protected surroundings, the number of animals often increases so rapidly that there isn't enough food to go around making it necessary for a few parks to actually hire hunters, to kill off some of the elephant population. Only time, money, and research can solve these problems. Without these solutions, there is a real danger that elephants will soon become as extinct as dinosaurs.

For a million years elephants and men have shared the earth. Man has hunted elephants for food and ivory. Elephants have built our cities, fought our battles, and made us laugh. We have prayed to elephant gods, told stories about elephant heroes, and described large things with elephant words like "jumbo," "mammoth," and "elephantine." There are elephant footprints all over our history. For thousands and thousands of years the elephant has served man well. Now it is time for man to return the favor.

Camerapix

The real African elephant's "graveyard"—hundreds of tusks piled in a warehouse prior to sale

WASHINGTON, May 9 (AP)—The Interior Department decided today that African elephants are not endangered, a move that some animal protectionists say spells doom for the world's largest land mammal.

—*The New York Times*,
May 10, 1978

Bibliography

Aelian, *On the Characteristics of Animals.* Translated by A. F. Scholfield. Cambridge: Loeb Classical Library, Harvard University Press, 1958.

Albion, Robert Greenhalgh, *Forests and Seapower: The Timber Problem of the Royal Navy 1652–1862.* Harvard Economic Studies, vol. XXIX. Cambridge: Harvard University Press, 1926.

Andersson, Charles John, *The Lion and the Elephant.* Edited by L. Lloyd. London: Hurst & Blackett, 1873.

Anonymous, "Okla. Elephant Hunt: Too Big to Handle?" *New York Post,* July 1975.

Anonymous, *The Elephant Principally Viewed in Relation to Man.* London: Charles Knight, 1844.

Bannerman, James, "The Tragical Death of the Great Jumbo." *MacLean's Magazine,* vol. 68, no. 23, Nov. 12, 1955, pp. 28–29, 43–50, 54.

Barnum, P. T., *Struggles and Triumphs.* Edited by George Bryan. New York: Alfred A. Knopf, 1927.

Beard, Peter H., *The End of the Game.* Garden City: Doubleday, 1977.

Benedict, Francis, *The Physiology of the Elephant.* Washington: Carnegie Institution of Washington, 1936.

Blond, Georges, *The Elephants*. New York: Macmillan, 1961.

Carrington, Richard, *Elephants: A Short Account of Their Natural History, Evolution, and Influence on Mankind*. London: Chatto & Windus, 1958.

Childe, V. Gordon, *Man Makes Himself*. New York: New American Library, 1951.

Coon, Carleton S., *The Story of Man*. New York: Alfred A. Knopf, 1954.

Cummings, Lewis V., *Alexander the Great*. Boston: Houghton Mifflin, 1940.

Darnton, John, "A Ban on Animal Trophy Sales Brings Last-Day Rush in Nairobi," *New York Times*, March 13, 1978.

Davidson, Basil, *A History of East and Central Africa to the Late Nineteenth Century*. Garden City: Doubleday/Anchor Books, 1969.

De Beer, Gavin, *Hannibal: Challenging Rome's Supremacy*. New York: Viking Press, 1969.

Deraniyagala, P. E. P., *Some Extinct Elephants, Their Relatives and the Two Living Species*. Ceylon: Government Press, 1955.

Dharmakumarsinhji, K. S., et al., *Wildlife Conservation in India: Report of the Expert Committee, Indian Board for Wildlife*. Dehra Dun: F.R.I. Press, Publicity and Liaison Branch Forest Research Institute and Colleges, 1970.

Douglas-Hamilton, Iain and Oria, *Among the Elephants*. New York: Viking Press, 1975.

Easton, Stewart C., *The Heritage of the Past*. New York: Holt, Rinehart & Winston, 1955.

Elwin, Verrier, *Myths of Middle India*. London: Oxford University Press, 1949.

Frazer, James George, *The Golden Bough, A Study in Magic and Religion*, abridged ed. New York: Macmillan, 1971.

Getty, Alice, *Ganesa, A Monograph on the Elephant-Faced God*. Oxford: Clarendon Press, 1936.

Holland, A. J., *Ships of British Oak*. Newton Abbot: David & Charles, 1971.

Jeannin, Albert, *L'Éléphant d'Afrique: zoologie-histoire-folklore-chasse-protection*. Paris: Payot, 1947.

Kipling, John Lockwood, *Beast and Man in India.* London: Macmillan, 1892.

Lamb, Harold, *Tamerlane.* New York: Robert M. McBride & Co., 1928.

Laws, R. M., I. S. C. Parker, R. C. B. Johnstone, *Elephants and Their Habitats: The Ecology of Elephants in North Bunyoro, Uganda.* Oxford: Clarendon Press, 1975.

Leidecker, Kurt F., *The Life of Buddha According to Thai Temple Paintings.* Illustrated by Rudolf Hampe. 1957.

Livy, *The War with Hannibal,* Books XXI–XXX of *The History of Rome from Its Foundation.* Translated by Aubrey de Sélincourt, edited by Betty Radice. Harmondsworth: Penguin Books, 1965.

Mackenzie, Donald A., *Indian Myth and Legend.* London: Gresham Publishing Co., n.d.

Marshall, H. N., *Elephant Kingdom.* London: Robert Hale, 1959.

Martin, E. Osborn, *The Gods of India.* London: J. M. Dent, 1914.

Moorehead, Alan, *The Blue Nile.* New York: Dell, 1968.

Noble, Margaret E., and Ananda K. Coomaraswamy, *Myths of the Hindus and Buddhists.* London: G. Harrap, 1914.

Pilkington, Cynthia, *Elephant over the Alps.* London: Macmillan, 1961.

Pliny, *Natural History.* Translated by Philemon Holland, edited by Paul Turner. Carbondale: Southern Illinois University Press, 1962.

Plutarch, *Lives.* Translated by John Langhorne and William Langhorne. London: J. Mawman, 1810.

Polybius, *The Histories of Polybius,* vol. I. Translated by Evelyn S. Shuckburgh. Bloomington: Indiana University Press, 1962.

Rawlinson, H. G., *India: A Short Cultural History.* Edited by C. G. Seligman. New York: D. Appleton-Century Co., 1938.

Rensberger, Boyce, *The Cult of the Wild.* Garden City: Doubleday/Anchor Books, 1977.

————, "This Is the End of the Game." *The New York Times Magazine,* Nov. 6, 1977, p. 38.

Sanderson, Ivan T., *The Dynasty of Abu.* New York: Alfred A. Knopf, 1962.

Scullard, H. H., *The Elephant in the Greek and Roman World.* Ithaca: Cornell University Press, 1974.

Sikes, Sylvia, *The Natural History of the African Elephant.* London: Weidenfeld & Nicolson, 1971.

Sillar, F. C., and R. M. Meyler, *Elephants Ancient and Modern.* New York: Viking Press, 1968.

Symes, Michael, *An Account of an Embassy to the Kingdom of Ava in the Year 1795*, 2 vols. Edinburgh: Constable & Co., 1927.

Werner, M. R., *Barnum.* New York: Harcourt Brace Jovanovich, 1923.

Williams, J. H., *Elephant Bill.* Garden City: Doubleday, 1950.

Williamson, George C., *The Book of Ivory.* London: Frederick Muller, 1938.

Index